THROUGH ROSE COLORED GLASSES

other books by the author

Poetry:
Dawn Visions
Burnt Heart/Ode to the War Dead
This Body of Black Light Gone Through the Diamond
The Desert is the Only Way Out
The Chronicles of Akhira
Halley's Comet
Awake as Never Before
The Ramadan Sonnets
The Blind Beekeeper
Mars & Beyond
Laughing Buddha Weeping Sufi
Salt Prayers
Ramadan Sonnets (The Ecstatic Exchange revised edition)
Psalms for the Brokenhearted
I Imagine a Lion
Coattails of the Saint
Abdallah Jones and the Disappearing-Dust Caper
Love is a Letter Burning in a High Wind
The Flame of Transformation Turns to Light
Underwater Galaxies
The Music Space
Cooked Oranges
Through Rose Colored Glasses

Theater / The Floating Lotus Magic Opera Company:
The Walls Are Running Blood
Bliss Apocalypse

Puppet Theater:
The Mystical Romance of Layla & Majnun
The Journey to Qalbiyya

Compilation of Quotes: Warrior Wisdom

Prose: Zen Rock Gardening
The Little Book of Zen
Zen Wisdom

THROUGH ROSE
COLORED GLASSES

poems

July 22, 2002 – January 15, 2003

Daniel Abdal-Hayy Moore

The Ecstatic Exchange

2008

Philadelphia

For quotes any longer than those for critical articles and reviews,
contact:
The Ecstatic Exchange,
6470 Morris Park Road, Philadelphia, PA 19151-2403
email: abdalhayy@danielmoorepoetry.com

First Edition
ISBN: 978-0-6151-8412-8 (paper)
Published by *The Ecstatic Exchange,*
6470 Morris Park Road, Philadelphia, PA 19151-2403

Acknowledgements and thanks to *Philadelphia Stories* and its 2007 anthology in
which the poem *The Piano Chord Most Adjacent to the Inexpressible* first appeared.

Also available from *The Ecstatic Exchange*, Knocking from Inside,
by Tiel Aisha Ansari

Cover and text design by Abdallateef Whiteman | www.ianwhiteman.com
Cover collage by the author
Back cover photograph by Malika Moore

بسم

DEDICATION
To
Shaykh ibn al-Habib
(and the continuation of the Habibiyya)
Shaykh Bawa Muhaiyuddeen,
all shuyukh of instruction and ma'arifa,
Baji Tayyaba Khanum

and my wife of constant heart
Malika

*The earth is not bereft
of Light*

CONTENTS

AUTHOR'S NOTE ABOUT THE TITLE

SOME REALISTS MAY object to looking *through rose colored glasses*, and indeed it is a true spiritual objective to see things clearly, unobscured by our fates (as Rumi says in his Mathnawi), or our gnarly emotions and peculiar selfhoods – especially if we insist, in a New-Agey Pollyanna mode, on seeing everything in the best, glass-half-full light no matter what.

These times of drastic and endless global tragedy call for extraordinary strengths. It seems our avenues of actual resistance to the evils around us are limited, though they may have always been, and at the same time the recourses to true and pure action, or impactful, salvational inaction, may have always been with us by God's Grace, sent via divinely inspired messengers, prophets and saints.

In the heady days of the 60s I had a theater company called *The Floating Lotus Magic Opera Company*, where we performed at night by torchlight in an outdoor amphitheater in North Berkeley, California, complex ritual dramas against the Vietnam War, intending to exorcise all war from the hearts and minds of mankind (an ambitious project), basing our chanted poetry choreographies loosely on Tibetan liturgy. We meditated in Zen fashion and always intoned a long and sonorous round of AUMS (peace) before each performance. The final phase of each play was volcanically and cathartically positive, and after an audience meditation came ecstatic singing. Some of the more radical street theater politicos considered this approach "airy fairy," but the energy in our productions was every bit as radical as theirs, and we always had huge audiences. It's just that our intentions were different.

My *modus operandi* then was based on the notion that instead of just reacting and rebelling against evils, we needed to emphasize pure and positive spiritual power, to offer a way out, to create an alternative and bearable reality rather than just hate and resist the bad, or as Ezra Pound ends his epically magisterial Cantos, after all its history and economics and lyricism, "*To be men, not destroyers.*"

In Bergman's 60s movie, *The Seventh Seal,* the main character, a medieval Crusader returning from war having lost all his faith, searches for a truth from everyone, but is filled with existential *angst* and disquiet while playing chess with Death on a stormy beach. But another character, a cheerful fool, a performing juggler who lives in a traveling wagon with wife and baby, has frequent visions of the Virgin Mary walking with the Christ Child in the woods, and is always ecstatically joyous, full of faith even in a land of plague and war, and totally free of doubt. He's all heart, where the Crusader is all wracked and harried mind.

I'm with the fool. I'm with William Blake, saying, "*If the Sun and Moon should doubt, They'd immediately Go Out,*" and, "*If the fool would persist in his folly, he would become wise.*" If it's a matter of accentuating the positive in our short lives, of having faith in the grip of disaster and desperation, of holding to it even while the world seems to be sinking in one disaster after another, with political madmen at the helm, and singing of it the way French poet Guillaume Apollinaire did in the First World War, seeing beauty even in the enemies' flares from his miserable foxhole, then yes, for our life is so short it's snuffed out almost before it's begun, and we have to "kiss the joy as it flies" to live in eternity's sunrise.

What Dante saw at the end of his journey was a vast revolving white rose of many tiers in the spectacular paradisiacal heavens on whose dazzling petals saintly ones of various stations were placed, in a radiance too overpowering, and ultimately too indescribable even to behold or hold onto, its evanescent vision at the point of vanishing like the aftermath of a dream: the rose of illumination, majestic glimpse of the Divine that stops words and drenches silence in meaning. So the rose is not just rosiness, not just a rosy floweriness, but an awesome illumination of God's Loftiness.

For Allah is always First and Last, eternally before every firstness and eternally after every lastness. And He (*Hu*, the unified, indefinitely gendered Arabic pronoun) is the Face of Truth and Light we've been inspired by the Prophet, peace of Allah be upon him, to see in every event, time after time, before, after and *during*, to seek His Face in *everything* we see – as if, with the heart's mirror polished, *through rose colored glasses.*

The Prophet Muhammad, peace and blessings of Allah be upon him, said, "Seventy-thousand or seven-hundred thousand of my followers (the narrator is in doubt as to the correct number) will enter Paradise holding each other till the first and the last of them enter Paradise at the same time, and their faces will have a glitter like that of the moon at night when it is full."

— NARRATED BY SAHL BIN SA'D
(SAHIH BUKHARI)

I   CHRIST STEPS DOWN

Christ steps down from a golden car onto a
lake covered with luminous berries

The silence is like silver next to black or a
hush from a mile away billowing toward us

The afternoon becomes neither sunlit nor overcast
neither morning nor evening

When he opens his gray eyes to look at us with their
gold pupils we see that his
weeping has stopped and his hands are
extending out over the world

The blue cape wrapped around his bare shoulders spreads like a
heron's wings about to take flight but then
falls in great folds around him again as he
walks forward
each step longer than the last until he is
standing before us

Those who would cut off his head at the
neck have fled to a far country
pursued by a black flame the exact shape
of themselves

He opens his lips to speak but we are
drowned in his face and there is
nowhere we have been now that is
left for us to go and even
space has shrunk from its unwieldy furniture and cloudy windows
to his pure dimension

Wolves circle the lake like ghosts
and their howling shakes the
air which has become moonlight

Christ releases us
into the rippling reflections that
ebb with the moonlit waters to the rounded shore
to become silhouettes of trees waving
tall against the night

7/22

2 THE DAY DEATH KNOCKED AND NOBODY ANSWERED

I

One day death knocked and no one answered
neither the chambermaid in her outdated pinafore wiping her
hands nor the boy with the
broken arm running out from the backyard nor even
the Russian gardener coming round the hedge
nor the Norwegian pianist putting the
final touches on his étude and swaying
back on his bench

Death knocked again and not even the
cat jumping down from the ledge nor the
crazy bicyclist daring to jump over the ramp and staying
suspended in midair for the count of at least
five

Neither the buzzer at the door nor the
pickles in the jar neither the
ants being probed by a spaniel nor the
last butterfly to leave the hutch

For some reason no mortal could fathom
death for the
first time in its life was going unanswered

It checked the address and knocked again
three times three and nine times nine it
knocked on the old oak door but everyone
went about their way and totally
ignored it

Undeterred death looked in a window
happy to see a flower wilt brown under its
gaze but

Human faces seemed unfazed and
looked past it to a distance somewhere else
in space

A sewing needle dropped to the floor
but it took a full five minutes in
slow motion to hit the wood with an
audible ping
which startled everyone but death

Who smiled a broad but chilly
smile as it saw through a door at the
end of a long corridor a man cross his
hands over his chest and
close his tired eyes at last

2

Poor death all alone eternal spinster
riderless horse pebble rainfall bucket of
ash window covered over with
bad tar paper lost sheet music sick
ticket preying on the living going
where you're not wanted
circus act fanfare and nothing happens
casting call for friends and relatives in room
1307 ICU
instant mugger on a dark street in a face stocking
nail driven sideways
unfillable shoes

3

Turns out he was just napping
death's secret lover
hands crossed over chest in preparation for the
Inevitable now knocking on the door
but unanswered

Where do giraffes go or birds?
With so many birds why don't we see millions of
dead bird bodies instead of just a
ghoulish ant-fleeced tiny matted
carcass or two usually cat-produced?

Do they simply keep flying one day past earth's
perimeters little porous air skeletons
flapping pointy wing-bones in the dark
or turn into pure soul in mid-flight
slowing dissolving into thin air?

Death knocked again through thin air
someone tilted his face
death looked intently
the household was bathed in a blue light
the people inside moved in life's well-placed movie lights
life's vivid reds and greens with sound coefficients in sync or out
life's seeming endlessness
like dozing crocodiles on a riverbank
their snouts above the mud and flowering
lotus bowls

Death dared to look away for a moment
and the household inside became white horses in stalls stomping
impatient hooves on wood planks chrysalis pods stuck to flower buds
gestures of vague smoke in various twist shapes moving from
room to room but carrying on
audible conversations in arcane Alsatian tongues

When it looked back again death was a
white face looking down from a
mountain peak a mixture of lunar beauty with golden inner glow
and goofy-smiling clown
eyelids heavy with contemplation

And instead of knocking it let its gaze glide
gracefully across the valley to the nestled village below

and closed its gorgeous topaz eyes
slowly over the world

7/22-23

3   THE MAGUS MEETS THE HOLY ONE

I

The twelve harps of Rhiannon sounded as the
magus entered the hall down shadowed
colonnade after colonnade and past
fountain after fountain through sumptuous
halls where tapestries displayed the victories of
battle with no blood spared for the
smiting of enemies

and treasures of beaten gold and tempered
steel of swords and captured halberds crossed over
doorways and wooden chests intricately carved from
Cathay as he

moved below the sunlight of open courtyards a
tiny figure in black cowl and cape
though on his own swift level he was
tall and stooped and his lined face from many
desert crossings could be traced like a map
this magus from among the original magi
now in an even more remote place even more
forgotten of men

entered the presence at last of the holy one
and found a child again this time seated
eyes open face lifting to him as he
entered mouth already speaking small
hands holding delicate objects
not held or supported by anyone else no one
in fact seeming to be anywhere near
the baby's face smiles at him as soon as he
enters and a little gesture indicates he should
sit down and the small light of this
dusk-filled room beams enough for each to
see each other's eyes glowing like coals
about to become diamonds
and the magus positions himself squarely before the
holy one in this room bare of any luxury or even
basic comfort the baby seated perfectly on
stone pale brown naked body
wrapped in light

2

The baby opened its mouth like a dawn field of
sunflowers and said
"If the arms of your chair enfold you
and your heart light as a feather falls into
any furthering updraft"

Then it gurgled and cooed and blew
bubbles like any baby until the magus grew
restless thinking he'd hallucinated it all out of the
deepest yearning of his soul
but as soon as he moved one sleeve one single inch
the baby's face again grew solemn and his tiny
eyes met his like a seasoned diplomat

"Your boat needs more oarsmen and your
river more water
your floods need more passionate drinkers and your
tribulations must bring you to your knees

and the sky will pull back its curtains
and God's horses pull back their lips to their gums
and evil pull back its troops of mounted
demons so we may
enter cities of light as we're meant to
in prosperous peace"

Suddenly the room filled with great whirling
white cloths and nursemaids appeared their
tiny chipmunk faces alert and pointed
and lifted the baby poised on the stone
and wrapped him in miles of fleecy down
until only his face showed
his gaze never leaving the fixed eyes of the magus
like the moon never losing its brightness in a
sky of moving clouds

"Take the arm of the oldest shepherd
take water from the oldest well
take footsteps that have gone before you
and erase your name from your eyes
until the world shows only its light to you
in all its glory and the world itself disappears in
all its glory and only a
sound remains in the space of utter silence
only a simple high-pitched sound
only a single name repeated by the waves of the air"

Then he was taken from the room
and all the walls turned red
and the floor opened out on a sheer cliffside from which
the magus clung

3

The cliff from which the magus clung
lasted only as along as a song is sung

Nothing lasts as long as it could
tribulation the shedding of blood

The sky became pewter and sang like a choir
his eyes saw the light that's central to fire

Expanding in waves across the world
above which his desperate fingers curled

Until he could hold to the cliff no more
and dropped through time and space to the floor

Of the holy one's chamber with its silver stars
in triangular circles in transparent jars

7/24-?

4 THE MYSTIC COIL

I

The cheese the divine cheese-maker makes
already has mice in it chewing nicely
all but one chew themselves out of it

and the mice already have cats around them
in the same way bubbling water in an alchemical flask has
glass around it

and the happy cats smiling with mice in their stomachs
have dogs' eyes burning intently in a circle around them
and have already shot up a tree with their hair on end and whiskers bristling
and the tall tree already struck by lightning is
afire with new leafy inspirations bursting with rays

and the lightning bouncing like two-year olds on the
turbulent gray mattress of the sky
is already broken up into its constituent positively and
negatively charged ions
and goes peacefully to sleep in a conjunction of clouds already
being blown across the ocean by a fierce nor'easter

and the ocean's waters are already being atomized and siphoned
up into the swiftly passing clouds and the

waters themselves are churned like giant cables by currents deeper than
thought itself as they braid their way toward the tropics

where coconut palms are already dropping their wooden footballs on the
heads of reptiles and colonialists out walking

to the cheese shop in town where the
cheese-maker is just now about to slice a
fresh wedge until he
notices a mouse tail sticking out one end as the
little curved doorbell jangles and the well-dressed
customer rubbing his bumped head enters

asking for a slice

2

We're born with our skeleton inside us
whom we'll meet on the road
pushing or not pushing a wheelbarrow full of
fashionable hats

The vistas and Venetian balconies we'll stand or not
stand on at sunset are there inside us as well

The voyage up or not up the Orinoco River to its
source the trip

taken or not taken to Louisiana at the
height of the Mardi Gras

The time past long before our birth and
long past our death is typed into our
blood by typists with otherworldly
alphabets seated on adjustable clouds

as we find ourselves in the court of
Alexander the Great wondering if he's really as
great as they say

or in the moonlight on a terrace 2000 years from this very moment
asking for grains of salt to be passed through the air in their
silver salt shaker the same as yesterday

3

The saint leans forward and looks into our faces
and all previous connections fall apart all
earlier associations so tightly woven unravel
and their bright threads elastically stretch over a new
dimension of the world carefully forgotten in the small blankets of
childhood folded away under a tree at the
edge of a forest of voices wrapping their
long branches forever around a mystery
made plain in the saint's eyes as he
gazes at us

and the huge camellia-like petals of the world unfurl to let us
enter a safe place at last
beyond our birth-dates and death-dates

on a road that neither slopes up nor down

but leads straight as light over a smoking gully in
nothing at all
surrounded by God's vast limitless Something

and leans forward even a little closer
and smiles

7/30

5 HE WANTED TO GO ON A LONG JOURNEY

He wanted to go on a long journey
so he closed his eyes and started
counting his breaths until he could see

the snowclad onion roofs of Moscow
the glistening fields of Fayyoum Egypt
the stifling downtown city congestion of Hong Kong
and he was happy swatting flies from his food
and stepping on passionflower thorns on the Island of Maui
he was happy setting off by train across Central Asia
sitting next to a shepherd in a
coat reeking of lanolin
he was happy listening under the stairs to the
Beethoven concert in Baden-Baden on period instruments

and then he got up and instead of
shooting himself with the little pearl-handled pistol in his belt
for the third night in a row
he opened the nearest window and a
star chariot leaned close and opened its
side door to let him enter

and following the map of Albertus Magnus
he lit up the corners of his beloved's love letters with a
fast blue flame that spelled out what his
vocabulary couldn't express

She awoke to a table set with small triangular toasts on
bone china plates and a little pot of
honey so transparent and golden
it transformed the spoon that ladled it into sheer ruby

and her lips into plump blueberries closing slowly over a
sky road of doves' flight over fields of
burnished silver

7/31

6   DELIRIOUS LIGHT

Ambrose Bierce was a merry old soul with a
fabulous name but I only know his
"Devil's Dictionary" so I
leave him alone

Harry Connick Jr. also has a name that sounds like a
tapdance step you might do before
getting into something really fast and complex

I've always liked the name Lorenzo Jones
though I don't remember who he is or was
seems like someone from my childhood
(I think a soap opera on 1940's radio)
but I know he wasn't Lentil
who played the harmonica when the
brass band couldn't because the sound of a
lemon being sucked by a meanie named Sneep
puckered their lips

Each root pebble snowflake stone damselfly and
cockroach of us has a name at least our
mother calls us
to hot dinners or angels do to a place in Paradise
reserved for no other

This world a place of direct personal involvement for
all concerned down to the slightest midge
though I wouldn't know its name exactly

Still as we fly along looking for a succulent leaf or two
in this exuberant garden
remembering everything has a God-given name somehow
bestows dignity where dignity is deserved

and gives illuminative structure to the
poppy fields that stretch before us
scintillatingly outlining each leaf-edge and blossom
with their delirious light

8/3

7 BUCKETS

Albertus Magnus is spending more and
more of his time fetching and carrying
He puts eels in his bucket and carries them uphill
He puts blocks of triangular wood in his buckets and
carries them to the end of the road
He puts sand in his panniers and hauls them over his
bare shoulders to the new building site
He puts rocks in his buckets and carries them to the
twisting road and throws them down the side
He puts deer food in his buckets and totes them
out to where the dark forest begins
He puts bird seed in his buckets one in each
hand and carries them to the bird platforms and pours it
carefully so each kernel gets eaten
He puts scrolls in a brass chest and heaves it
onto his head and walks unsteadily at first
down the long road
He puts knives and hammers in a box and puts the
box in his bucket and hoists a
shovel over his left shoulder and sings a
tune as he walks
He puts bushels of golden wheat in his
buckets and they
sparkle in the sunlight

He puts pure golden sunlight in both panniers and it
weighs the pans equally so that when he
walks to the top of the hill with his
arms and neck aching but his
face glowing
the day itself catches fire from the
light and shines like a diamond gleam in
God's eye showering slants
from its divine facets onto whatever in creation
come-what-may
both before him and after him `
and everywhere around him

8/4

8   THE SLOPE OF THE MOUNTAIN

The slope of the mountain is its gift to us
or else it would be perfectly sheer

The lightning-storm clattering this way and that
with its quicksilver electronic bolts
is a peace signature when the sky clears

Wheels rotating faster than the eye can see
like the nearly invisible velocity of minnows
is their utter stillness in the two
worlds with silent reverberations in both

The madman who swings an axe in the marketplace
running amok after a mild-mannered lifetime of
niceties and simple courtesies is the
world cleaved in two and each radiant
half like a wound translated into two
foreign languages both expressing pain

The end of the world takes place in a
breath-beat before the beginning
its chorus of blind singers on rooftops
serenades every tragedy that ever befalls us
like teams of horses falling
gradually through the air their eager
destination thwarted

The sign of sound is its careful articulation
a gasp instead of a shout a crying out in
high-C instead of a low croon in a
cheap dive

I kiss the back of the hand of the initial impetus
I stroke the living flame into a blaze from a
lone spark in the heart put there
personally by Divine gesture

We shall not have lived in vain if we can
see this in the blink of our life that we've
been given shedding
radiant hairs blindingly bright
a sweet embrace on a mountain slope
in a lightning storm that's over faster than the
rotation of wheels like a controlled madness
brought home in the glance of a loving eye
somewhere just before the fierce

dawn of the world

8/5

9   BACK GARDEN AT 62

Like my little row house backyard garden
even though I'm now 62
I'm just starting out
each year a new profusion of green
vines grasses weeds of particular beauty Black-eyed Susans from
before clumps of reeds shoots of brown whatevers

This year particularly beautiful a real
secret grotto garden as I'd so
desired where a Rousseau tiger might prowl
bamboo-slatted cyclone fence on three sides
giant burst of bright golden yellow Black-eyed Susans on the right
a little plot of grass I keep cut short in the
middle only about five yards long and
three yards wide but a
velvety green and in the
middle of all these leafy green hues
a bright white plastic K-Mart birdbath along Greek classical lines
where mostly wasps drink though I saw two
English Sparrows dip and sip its waters this afternoon then
fly off to the brick apartment houses across the alley

In the same way I too feel profuse with
sunlight pouring through variegated
shapes and dimensions

strange creeping vines wrapping those Braille-reading
tendrils around the back of the white metal
patio chairs and up the red bricks of the
back wall on sticky salamander finger-pads

and two new maple trees bravely
beginning perhaps a long day on earth
one about eight feet tall the newest I
planted myself from the front walk
now up to my thigh

and I hope I am always also open to the sky
and available to hungry birds in their
quick fidgety flocks one now

singing extra loud over teenage neighborhood calls from the
next street over and an airplane full of
people making its way out of sight from
somewhere far away to somewhere near

bright clouds but with dark gray undercarriages
hopefully no barrier

8/7

10 THREE ANGELS IN MY BACK GARDEN

One day three angels came into my back garden and
stared at me through the window
one was red one was black one was yellow
and their voices sounded like bells

They stood as a trio of lights trembling in the air
their gazes were purple beams so fine
they were more like ultraviolet rays
but then their gazes became molecular highways through the normal
and anything might travel on them to my door

The three angels rippled expectantly though didn't gesture for me to
join them nor refuse that possibility
we simply existed in two spaces separated by a window
that would otherwise be one
me inside the house looking out
they in the backyard garden surround by variegations of green
looking in

And while this wasn't actually a vision or
visitation it was an inspiration in
words that came unbidden and opened a
viewing perspective in my imaginal mind
bubbles up from the heart animating it
then the mind figuring out or waiting for an explanation of
who they were or what they did which was
faithful to a reality that not only
could have happened there on the grass in the

shadows of the fence under blue sky
but actually did and is still happening in these
written lines as they turn to form a circle of
sparkles almost disappearing as they
rotate hand in hand their long bright
Technicolor peacock-feather wings
whisking through the air making truly exotic flowers
bloom to firework fullness as they turn I didn't even know were
there until

some of the sky descends and the earth seems to
bend upward as if for a kiss
and the three angels all turn their faces once more to
look at me and now've become more
glance than features more eye light than
physical delineation until actually they've
disappeared altogether leaving only the
garden scintillating with an unbeforeseen
brightness described now where
before each leaf and tendril-curl existed in its
own light each grass blade trembled in breezes

Now the garden is brought to life by
an ecstatic exhalation of amber-hued breath so vast
each whale in creation inhales it as it surfaces and
circulates it through its huge bulk as it dives back
into sea darkness

thankfully serene

8/8

11 FIRST THE KNEES GIVE OUT

First the knees give out then the
ship's rudder then the bank account then the canary cage
then Uncle Henry's moustache then the tablecloth begins to
fray the chair falls apart doors fall off their hinges the
cows start speaking in tongues the
eyes blur our food turns back to its
origins in the earth or on the hoof
the sky itself begins to look old as it has
never before usually perennially adolescent or even
in its eternal baby-blue infancy
trees begin to produce purses full of play money
hills begin to growl like overheated engines as they
start their climb
everyone else looks positively glamorous in black and
white or color

and so it goes as time goes by

waving one moment from a quick window
or being the one waved to
as everything actually revolves around
time's immovable pivot

water falling backwards into the awed mouth of the
river from which it flowed

8/11

12 MY MOTHER

I don't think my mother knew what I was
talking about half the time
it felt like I was playing one game and
she was watching another
the ball might fly straight up in the air
but she'd see a square orb being jacked up like a
house or else wonder how much the ball cost

Was she a miniature goddess enshrined in a painted ostrich egg
holding magical implements and making a
secret empowering sign with her hands?

A small mouth that held words from the library
whose kisses though Victorian were sweetly sought
but thunder cracked above her head when I was
born and there was no time before that
in which I was conceived
it was all a gray ocean with no shores
it was all a sky of green birds around an
earth like a floating pearl in a giant oyster of blackness
nothing shook its calm and the sky extended for
light years before hitting another material body

My mother sat on a stone lion
and chose the sandwich of the day
green pepper on pumpernickel
soft cheese on hard tack
tuna fish with walnuts on white bread

and multitudes benefited from her choices
though she was fast asleep when their
haggard faces turned to her in gratitude
she was already elsewhere writing
checks to charities and sitting in on a
foursome for Bridge

Photographs show a slight woman with a
slightly ski nose and melancholy
eyebrows a dimpled chin and winsome smile

In the forties she wore odd hats with
little stiff veils in front and shoulder pads on her
suits dressed up to go nowhere
now she's dressed the wild hills of Oakland themselves
with the fine lace of her ashes strewn
and the wind that may pick up a microscopic
flake or two will never
reconstitute her bodily form elsewhere
the island she inhabits now has never been
discovered and the two wingéd white horses she
looks after have no hooves that
reach the ground and the

seasons steadfastly refuse to change from
halcyon and bright where she is
and there is no chill and no heat wave
where she is

and her hand extended now from there to
where I am right now
has a ring with a tiny moon on it
silently winking its name
which I can just make out in its
bare rudiments from time to time
when I write out these poems

8/13

13 MY FATHER

My father on the other hand taught me how to
sharpen a knife on a Carborundum stone
a little spit or 3-IN-ONE oil and a
clockwise circular motion with the
knife edge tilted just so until a kind of
inky residue is made and the blade becomes sharp as
paper

and he secretly wrapped himself in his Masonic cloak
and Shriner's red felt fez with tight embroidery
insignia of sphinx face and scimitar in gold wiry
thread in front and would float through the
rooms of the house in double-breasted blue serge
suit and conservative tie and Brylcreamed
hair off to some secret somewhere unbeknownst to the
unworthy rest of us even though bonafide
family members sadly uninitiated in the arcane arts

My father had wooden slats he peered through at us
he sounded like metal rivets walked on by
rubber-soled shoes in search of game
only his game were pheasant and salmon
his was a game I couldn't play
and he looked sternly over the fence of that
impossibility at me as I
stretched myself on canvas on the attic floor and pretended to
fly

He beetled his black eyebrows up and
down as in a silent movie
a blue wind of secrecy and commerce blew him along
and may continue blowing him between
tall buildings even today in whatever
Paradise I hope he inhabits with my
mother who could never really
manage well on her own except by
polite smiles and patient necessity

He passes in an armored car he walks by in a
hurry surrounded by blue flames to the office where his reality dimension
takes material shape beyond what we can
ever see or understand
and even though I resemble him more and
more as I grow older no matter what I do
our wings are different our flight patterns
diverged somewhere around age fourteen for me
and the speck in the sky I saw
diminish from then on surrounded by its
own halo followed a trajectory I know
nothing about in this life of ours

My father having spermed me into
existence then stood by to witness my peculiar independence
in a sky filled with nocturnal birds
and stars a little too blurred for
sure and knowledgeable navigation

8/13

14 TO SEE THE END BEFORE THE BEGINNING

I

To see the end before the beginning and the
prince before the toad and the

snapshot before the pose and the fence before any
land has been ceded

the kiss before the meeting on this side before
the dream has even delineated the

shape of the main characters' faces and bodies
the eyelash caught on the eye's glistening emulsion before the

existence of the eye itself comes formally into
being to view the universe all the way to where our

solar system ends and interstellar space begins
through the pupil of the eye that

beholds it reflected from a pewter mirror
salvaged from Pompeii even before a

whiff of sulfur announces the volcano's
presence the ecstatic purity of being in its

soap-clear nakedness before names turn like
tiny darts toward the things they name

and shoot through time and space to their
enunciated targets all before

anyone capable of enunciating them
can open their lips for the first time with

tongue poised against teeth to perfectly pronounce the
word "*foot*" or "*rose*" or "*halfway*" or "*you're on fire!*"

2

To see the end before the first microbe has
ventured out past the marsh's dark shadow
in a blaze of bright green sunlight

Each moment it's the end and beginning coiled
tightly in each other's embrace and
staring each other down through beetling fiery
eyes as they turn in wheels along edges thin as paper

In each unfolding from an origin is our end
in each end is a paper lantern ready to catch fire
to illuminate the rocky mountain path
full of shaggy white crag goats that leads to our
sweet salvation just beyond the impossible pinnacle

from which we can survey the layout down below that
perfectly explains the contortions that got us here
and why some contortions still face us once we
reach the side of safety

but lamplight lights the corners of our faces now
and the shadowed crevices

until we resemble not so much ourselves
as we do fruit trees just at that springtime moment when
blossoms turn to succulent fruit and their fragrances
intoxicate even the drowsiest bees

8/15-16

15 LOVE AND DEATH

I

Love and death is always on his mind
love because water flows downward from a height
death because the white horse that crosses the road in
front of him is blind

Love because looking into the eyes of people is too dazzling
like looking at a night sky full of stars
death because he hears mice inside his walls
squealing and scampering and then nothing

Love because the way the world opens its fruit to him
pulling aside skin and pulp to show the amazing seed chamber
inside flooded with sunlight brings him
to tears
death because three black dwarves on bicycles are crossing a
tightwire over Niagara Falls blindfolded singing
arias from Puccini

Love because the eyelid of death pulls down over
everything but inside it is an Ode to Joy clear enough that
everyone can sight read it and burst into song
death because love wears a perfume from somewhere from
somewhere but you can't put your
finger on it you just can't quite
put your finger on it

2

He thinks about love the way a tree branch
actually and miraculously ends in a
twig with a perfect leaf formed on it
veins and stems and membrane for
photosynthesis

He thinks about death the way a fox
leaps in the snow after a rabbit its
eyes like laser beams and its sense of smell so
heightened it can smell fear

He thinks of love as boats plow through each other's
wakes on the high seas with the
sharp brass blade of the sun come down clean on a
misty horizon

He thinks about love the way someone with
piles of unopened love letters is just about to
open the first one after being in a coma in a
foreign country for fourteen days then
fluttered his eyelids and spoke her
name first thing

He thinks about death in an empty house
the rooms echo when you move through them
but outside in crystal-clear photo-sharp light is the
garden with topiary hedges and lakes full of Koi

He thinks about love on a hillside above a
funeral cortege where three coffins are being carried to a
true martyr's graveyard
who died of love not suicide who loved Allah so
much they forgot themselves and flickered like moths
until nothing was left but the
light they longed for

He thinks about love and death the way a
mother worries over her newborn
even when she's grown

And like a cork he rises and falls into the
air waves earth waves divine light waves
that circulate around everything
in this perilous night

8/17-18

16 THE DARK BLUE-GREEN LIGHT

The dark blue-green light of dawn out the window
showed a strange pointed elfin pinnacle like some

far off Nordic scene in some
heavy primordial mist

which turned out to be the large dark green
garden umbrella

down

8/19

17 THE PIANO CHORD MOST ADJACENT TO THE INEXPRESSIBLE

The piano chord most adjacent to the inexpressible is the
one that dissolves into flocks of flying birds

The tree as it moves through the breeze most
adjacent to conducting the sonorous
filaments of the air stands as tall as a
doorman to an entranceway to the eternal mysteries

The desert most adjacent to spiritual enlightenment is the
one whose dunes yesterday don't resemble its
dunes today and whose dunes today
have slopes and dips totally ocean-like and unlike any of its
dunes tomorrow

The rain is finally falling after a month of drought
little earth-lips opening to drink in each drop
and the song each water-drinking element sings
resembles the chorus of an ancient opera sung among
cataclysmic rocks above tumultuous seas

There are no people in this poem
they are either asleep or haven't been born yet
but the sound in the landscape most adjacent to the
deep heartfelt human voice
is the night-cricket seeming to long for a mate wherever
it may happen to hear its lament repeated
incessantly but melodiously through the dark

So like us
in catastrophe or anti-catastrophe
calling out to space from our centrifugal loneliness
with a voice most adjacent to the
silent nuzzling feeler to feeler of ants meeting from
opposite directions
and lights beaming from north and south and brightly
blending somewhere over the
Arctic in a purple and scarlet shivering aurora borealis
whose ripples are most adjacent to the
music of the spheres hanging down into the
visible from the invisible heavens whose

radiant flowing draperies curving through the folding air
they are

8/23

18 WITHOUT STOPPING

Without stopping to check myself arrange my
feet make sure my
heart is beating on time
lift my face to the usual stars
crack my knuckles drum my fingers on
polished mahogany
make sure my trouser-seams are straight my
shoes polished and my hair properly aligned
I want to sing until my lungs flame outside like
iridescent sails like those incandescent
gossamer ash bags in Coleman Lanterns capable of
lighting up an arc of the woods against bears

In other words *O pulse O leap of faith O*
let's be done with shy betrayals

in other words
body decaying right before my eyes while a
whole aviary of sleek white birds inside is
chafing to be set free

in other words
this tongue of love like a living bridge like a
leaping flame to lick the moon

Let its reach extend and my eyes close in
peace let this frame hold a picture that has
none of me in it but all of light even if
only for an instant quicker than even a
fast photograph can capture

A door slam on what was
and the green reality of what is

studded with radiant spheres

8/24

19 NEITHER BRIDLED BY REINS

Neither bridled by reins with wet flanks
restless in foam
nor shackled in iron chains on ankles and wrists like
mutant ghosts forced to labor and
prized for muscle power (but not so long ago
some were)

Neither held together with baling wire nor
activated by electrodes or elevated scaffolds
nor drawn upright by magnetism from a
prone position in a blaze of purple light accompanied by
soft snare-drums and mysterious violin music

But also nor wafted satin ribbon above halcyon canyons
nor puffy clouds of giant mist or wisps of incense aloft across valleys
nor dragon-winged nor jet propelled nor aquatically dimensional
accelerating liquidly like squid or jellyfish boneless in the brine

But held in the embrace of skin-covered mortal physical form for an
imponderable duration in an upright position
passing the salt and hammering small nails into wood
and thanking the hosts and wishing for
peace and well-being for all

Sitting standing and massaging
finger-bones and saying goodnight and

going through doors and lying horizontal on
beds then sitting up again when our long sleep is
over

Neither all animal nor all angel

but light-sockets in blue pewter

with voices God uses to call the

farm hands to dinner

8/26

20 ALONG WITH THE REST OF US

I look at the shape of a moth and see the continent of Asia

I hear the high sawing of cicadas and hear
dot-dash star-scrape in outer space

I feel my feet on the earth and think I'm riding on an elephant
though in some cosmologies I might be riding on an
elephant who's standing on a turtle's back who's
balancing on a porpoise's nose who's got one flipper down
teetering on a sphere of golden light

There's a constant hum in the air or else in the
physicality of our inner ears
like electrical currents or a spatial ocean or just
mellow aliens communicating to each other via
human vessels and we're just
tuning in to their – to us – wordless conversation that might be
"Here comes a tidal wave sloshing at these
shores hmmmmm how strange and beautiful!"
or it might be a grocery list
"Twenty humans and a goat plus some
butter and a loaf of bread"

I write on paper in my 2 a.m. notebook
imperishable thoughts in imperishable images

but it might be a somewhat solidified cloud vapor
and I'm writing vapor onto coagulations of
mist-atoms and the next moment
it's all gone

along with the rest of us

8/29

21 ROSES

Roses – you let them into your house
with their raw and savage beauty
you put them in a cobalt bottle to set their
bright reds and delicate pinks against the
dark of night

They stand on tiptoe on their stems unfolding brash
petals from a secret center fortressed by thorns
you leave the serrated leaves as an Elizabethan
collar around them then count the
days of freshness as they
decay before your eyes from prized and nameless
gorgeousness to a puddle of petals at the
cobalt bottle's base

forced to see decrepitude with a snarl
the roses having entered your portals in
disguise
waving their best satins and crinolines
but they soon show
long teeth and the brown display of an
empty throne above piled snowdrifts of death

They strew their death before you on your path
they shower you with dry curled corollas

they present you with the wedding to which you must
so cheerfully or despondently go and

then count the aromatic hours with their pale
delicate hands

8/31

22 A LITTLE PEEK

A little peek over the fence is enough to convince us
A little glance at the center of igneous crystal
A short squint at how flame originates without even
going into phlogiston for explanation but a
short direct perception as its
liquidly licking flammable tongue takes over

A shy encounter with the green glow that takes
place in the womb at the moment of conception
the holy radiance that halos its harmonious spray of
high-pitched voices there

A blink just once at the thunderous core of a
dark icy light no bigger than a
gnat's eyelash but whose uncoiled spiral could
light the Arctic sky for a millennium if
unleashed raw like a stampede of
mythical beasts across the sky whose
silhouette alone would eclipse the moon

Even a blurred half-shut eyelid's worth of
galactic eyewitnessing of almost
motionless rotation that encompasses our
solar system and a billion others like
bubbles on the surface of boiling water if all those
bubbles each also had a billion
multi-hued bubbles coming to boils inside them
which also had etcetera bubbles each

one of which illuminates from incandescent core
outwards through cavalcades of bright lights and
glamorous bells ringing in slow-motion into a
hush of silence never approximated except perhaps in the
exact middle of a sound stasis hovering over the
Dead Sea or above a desert that seems to have
no end in sight and no sound apprehensible by
human ear apparatus

Even a quick examination of any of these
convinces us beyond words or designations

Convinces the part of us that's actually
already convinced where no amount of
philosophy adds or detracts but we become like a

string of early summer fireflies happily
flickering above garden greenery at
sunset for the first time all year

As if our glow could approximate what we've
seen that should convince even the most
stone-hearted of us having seen with our own eyes

the loquacious spark enlarge its luminous spectrum
to the sound of rapid harp-plucks

the light no bigger than a sliver that
turns from velvet black to all this
lit material perspective with no seeming
intermediary but just illumination itself

that descends upon someone by mysterious decree
and the whole process becomes discernible in the
glint of a saintly eye
who's seen it all directly

and has come to sing of it in our presence to
reconvince us of its light

9/2

23 WORDPLAY

The dozen roses I carefully cut and
placed in the box
did what roses must after all be famous for
they rose up and marched
themselves back to their beds

The butterflies also finally became
true to their name and shaped like
miniature railroad ties bright yellow
sticks of butter flew prettily above the
roses tucked into their beds
fluttering buttery wings careful not to
drip in the heat of the sun

A dog dogged my steps aware it was
God spelled backwards

A deer was just that
poignant on its hooves and innocent face and
huge eyes and it
endeared itself to my heart dear thing

I shall not mention the dragonfly
enlarged over the pond in its
ring of fire smoke belching from its body
frightening the forest folk

Nor the damselfly this one in fact a
damsel-in-distress-fly young darling in
tattered skirt being flown away with
little high-pitched squeals and I
think she was waving a hankie

A caterpillar meowed on its pedestal
preening its whiskers up there perched like an anchorite

A hummingbird ran through some old
Cole Porter tunes never once
opening its beak

A Cardinal blessed some English Sparrows
at the bird feeder as they
sat on a perch

9/4

24 TWILIGHT

You can really see what twilight's all about when you
try to continue reading and the ocular
cataracts of patchy darkness begin to
obscure the page and turn the
black print into little vague incandescences but
become almost illegible in the process

A battleship storms into the harbor to do
battle but enters a canyon of fog so
dense it can't see to shoot

A love letter gets so soaked with tears its
writing becomes rivulets of unreadable sobs

This page itself on our little patio table at
dusk is becoming so gray and
indefinite that I'm already writing more or less
automatically like a
blind man hoping for later legibility
the symbols' code broken into scrutible messages
wondering if ancient Egyptians or Mayans knew
that centuries later we'd try to shed
light of day and twenty-twenty
vision on their immensely secretive messages that were
probably to them as plain as day

9/7

25 THE MOTIONLESSNESS OF TIME

Waiting for
time to pass is like
sitting under a waterfall waiting for the
drops to land

A house at a tilt on a round hill

Sunlight fills the lined-up jam jars on the windowsill

Outside the door cricket racket sounds like
mechanical metal nets taking in netfuls of
flipping mechanical fish

You don't expect to make sense with a poem like this –
that would be too great an expectation

Ah – the motionlessness of time stands like a
solid roar up there at the
end of the road

9/9

26 WRITTEN IN FOUR WATCHES OF THE NIGHT

I

One line before lights out
one line in the dark

Which has more eternity in it
light or dark?

Red T-shirt wafted by the oscillating fan
body both bulky and slim
eyes completely mine I look out of
massive gelatinous consciousness back of them
I imagine partakes of the laciest galaxies as they
slowly spin

There's a bear somewhere snatching salmon out of a stream

There's a moose somewhere standing gigantic on a mountain

One line before lights out turned out to be
more like fourteen
but it's lights out now and the all
encroaching dark
to spin me in

2

OK I slept I woke
room basically the same as before
night outside screen door noises of crickets and cicadas
baroque rhythm section titillatingly sexy to another
insect

I dreamt but can't recall what dreamt
only that it was full-color episodic
the theme is lost the mere fact persists
sadly true of some lives I think
ignoring the theme of expansion investigation gaining
wisdom and exclaiming praise to the Holy Isolate One Alone
for each breath taken

fully the outbreath to the end and even to the end of the
end where the void lies for some or God's
plenitude for others then it
loops and we're inhaling all the way from
that far extended extreme to now way down
inside us filling lung-sacs with
such glorious ovules of air or whatever they might
be I think of them now as eyes looking about
in the dark the interior dark
which is where I'm switching the
light to right now

The enveloping nurturing dark

3

Which has more eternity in it
light or dark?

Light's on now pricking out each material detail
around before and above and below me
things crooked things aligned things piled things
hanging from the walls or stacked end to end

Somehow eternity yawns its lovely yawn here as well as
out in the curl of galaxies in pitch darkness
where there's no end in sight and you might
gasp at God's greatness

Here it's in spaces between spaces and
integers between integers as well as the
integers themselves and space itself

in which a clock might tick because it's a
clock and it must

but oddly independent of eternity simply
doing its clock thing

4

A dozen deer at the side of a forest
all heads alert in the same direction all eyes like black pools
all noses quivering flanks quivering hearts beating
awaiting a signal to stay still or go as
fast as their long legs can carry them
a world inside each one of them
their doe childhoods their antlered adolescences
their fates

The eternal part of us sees life pictures
all around us as these
bodies including ours come and go
like so many sheaths down over
Paradise

A marble rolls until it stops on earth's
gravitational pull or against a
material obstacle

Our eyes fill with light or dark
our hearts as well

One foot in front of the other
with millions of miles all around us

Do we stay still or go as
fast as our chair legs will carry us?

The learning curve loves us more than life does

Love loves us more than life does

The rope we grasp of it
is personal to the touch

9/17

27 GHERKINS

I

Little miniature pickles packed close together in a
bottle of brine *gherkins* I think they're called
or those miniature corns on the cob at cocktail parties
or the actual flea circus city with its
gray and blue houses and City Hall I saw on a
fairground in Mexico City in the 60s

A way of looking at the world or at our life
say through the wrong end of a telescope in order to
bring some detachment some distance to the things of our
existence so we won't be so encroached upon
they won't be so in our face
as if we were struck with *"reductivitis"* a new
rare disease that makes everything seem
small but actually I
don't think that's quite it at all
it's just to give us some breathing room

To not see the world as violent and as ill-bred as it
seems to be day after day in spite of our
best intentions

To not see our own lives as flies fallen into the
ointment with our wings stuck and our legs in the air
flailing for purchase

Yet we're not Lilliputians either
we can't just tie the boats together and pull them to
shore like Gulliver did

2

Then there's *"panorama-vision"* where every
action can be seen as taking place in front of a
magnificent and majestic natural or epic backdrop
the greeting of a friend as the meeting of
those railroads from east coast and west coast when they
drove the golden spike and posed for a celebratory
Daguerreotype

A love-tryst at an outdoor café table set before the
Himalayan peaks or in the dark rich iron-red depths of the
Grand Canyon at sunset

A whisper in an amphitheater of silver-white clouds

A sigh listened to by divine consciousnesses from an ancient era
when sighs meant whole hieroglyphic walls of
flame-lit meaning

Or a secret kept in the rift of the Carlsbad Caverns
in a dripping grotto icy cold bathed in
coral and emerald light and giant whale-rib formations
eye-glances in Paradise

Between disembodied souls at peace
at an oasis of delicate nectars

neither giant nor miniature creatures making
giant or miniature actions exactly but held by
greater Hands than ours
and breathed by a Breather Who both
precedes and follows us in a rhythmic anti-stasis

like a boat on the high seas that
knows it's human though surrounded by pitch-black night
heading toward a cordial shore

firefly in a bottle
pulsatingly emitting light

9/20-21

28 THE BODY'S MAJESTY

After exhaustion I extend my body out
and feel its majestic span

in the tired muscles and tendons a rush of a
feeling I can only say is majestic somehow

not me majestic exactly though in some states that
also could be said

bridge-girders in the backbone extension-bridge especially in the
spine that great and terrible transmitter throughout the

body that divine telegraph that if crushed or tampered with
shuts the whole body down

to the ends of my toes throughout the pleasurable achiness
from which white cranes took off as I

stretched and browsing water buffalo could be
spotted with vines dripping out their mouths lifting their

massive heads to blink at me from
labor's marshes

All these flashes as I extend my body for a
moment of rest disembedding themselves in
fragrant imageries floating off into space

but it was a magnificence there in the
flesh and bone I felt that is
not mine and is mine at the same time

a worthy sentient land mass for moonlight to land on
or a body worthy for the sun to make its
royally majestic arc above as it

moves through our daily sky

9/23

29 THERE'S NO COMFORT IN THIS WORLD

"There's no comfort in this world"
says the bear to the rabbit cornered by the
fox caught in the
cross-hairs of a Remington semi-automatic

"The ripe walnut spends more breaths on grief"
says the rabbit without breaking a sweat

"Large waters large waters large waters"
says the fox licking his lips

"I've got him!"
says the rifleman as the aneurysm starts its attack from a
blood clot in his leg

"Why do fat people laugh more than skinny people?"
says the aneurysm as a laser beam from
God's Throne stops it in its tracks

The rifleman thinks of his mother and her
deathbed wish and the tears in her eyes
and her last diary entry
and drops his gun

The fox gets distracted by a butterfly and lopes off on the
trail of a pungent odor of fresh pheasant
though it's all in his mind

The rabbit twitches pink nose and white ears
puts paws back on earth and hops off
tail wiggling looking for lunch

The bear glances around for a second
then calls after the rabbit as it
disappears into the brush

"*The ice-gates of Mercy melt open in the heart of the moment*"
and studies his snout in the puddle rain made on the ground
before shambling off into the woods

his stomach growling

9/24

30 HEY I'VE SKIDDED RIGHT OFF THE PLANET

Hey I've skidded right off the planet
now I'm hiding behind the clouds
like the sun

Seems the traction wasn't so good
maybe they polished it

Sure looks good from here like the
round button on a Chinese Emperor's jacket
all jade and turquoise and silver against black

God's bristly tickle can be felt all the way to here
a shivery kind of feeling of closeness and
impending divine invasion
of a king knocking down a fortress that's only
one person

Me

Back home on earth I was either reviled ignored or praised
and like pebbles into water my surface reacted with
circles and ripples for all three

Not that anyone noticed

If it should ever be time to go back again
I wonder what I'd like to be

a cloth wiping sweat off a saint's forehead

the window a prophet looks out of

the shadow cast by an angel across a valley of farms

But I'd probably be the lying lion who comes home
with lamb on his breath

the ring tossed into a hat by a gambler

the clearing throat of someone about to declare bankruptcy

I think I'll just stay here behind my cloud
and watch the horse teams flow past like an
ocean of white legs and manes

It's over in a second anyway
before we've got all the pictures pasted in
and just as we're beginning to get good
everything's left unfinished

God wants it that way

He'll finish us in His time
like someone reaching for a lift out of water
and being held by the sky

The bright nothing on the inside melts into the
bright nothing on the out

And the bright nothing in between
never existed anyway

9/25

31 THE DEW ON THE LIP

Dew on the lip of a sacred plant

Planet made less by the loss of an ant

Antenna that takes in the orbits of stars

Staring at space till it shows us its scars

32 CAN YOU IMAGINE STUFFING A MOSQUITO?

Can you imagine stuffing a mosquito?

Well I can

Can you imagine the perfect tear fallen on the
bodice of Anne Boleyn as the
axe cleans off her head from her neck in the dour dungeon?

Well there you are

Can you imagine the interior of a black thread or a white thread?

Can they be different?

Can you imagine the actual face and voice of Van Gogh and the
searing look of sincerity and desperation in his
eyes as he crosses a lane on his way home
a masterpiece under his arm?
The exact look the exact sound of his voice?

Well that's as near as we'll get

Can you imagine the thoughts of an alchemist as he feels he's
gotten closer to gold?

Can you imagine Harpo Marx's voice? Garcia Lorca's? Hart Crane's?

Can you imagine the actual moves Nijinsky
made in his prime the leaps the entrechats or even more
daring the dance he actually danced after sitting silent on a
chair in front of the audience for
a half hour and then said *"Now I will dance the war*
which you did not prevent and for which
you are responsible"?

Lost things to us forever however hard we try to imagine them

Can you see back behind time to your great
grandparents on the prairie say trying to stay alive
or *their* grandparents in the homeland trying to
emigrate to peaceful shores?

Can you imagine eating a human leg on Donner Pass?

I can't

Or being the first to see a white man coming through the
trees in pith helmet and khaki shorts and loaded musket?

I'd rather not

Or how the bay waters looked
as the Vikings headed into shore or more
enigmatically Irish monks in their
one-man leather boats after rough Atlantic crossing a
mystic's prayer on their lips and in their
hearts the whole time?

To hear murmurings as a
twittering of small birds or a fluttering of
moth's wings as in the music of Ravel?

Can you imagine the human imagination
turned somehow inside-out so what is
initially curious to us appears as awesome in
scope and dimension to its true measure

as the Prophet said of God *"I didn't
measure You with Your true measure"*

And across its dips and divides and glistening glades
fabulous creatures run as freely as wild horses
some with wings and some with human faces
through canyons of ecstatic bliss which wind along
rivers of milk and honey forever to a music so
exalted no man-made instruments could
approximate it and no human voice sound
any of its registers

As the dome of the sky opens up to ring above ring of
illuminated circles of angels of fiery color and gorgeous
light in no way misty or bland but as

bright and clearly delineated as blossoms on a
summer's day covered with dew-beads only their real

otherworldly appearance utterly defies our imaginations

and every one of our mental speculations

9/27

33 SIMPLE REBELLIOUS PARTICLES

Simple rebellious particles are separated
out from the main body and
conveyed on a belt to the
Particle Plantation for replanting

They thrive there sprayed daily by
sweet waters until they begin to have a
pulse of their own a kind of
particularized heartbeat
and are warmed by special rays until all
inflexibility and self-righteousness is removed

They are then released into a bath of algae-like
plants where they begin to breathe new air and with
a new kind of fullness
the main body feels more buoyant without them
and suddenly is capable of marvelous feats it had
great difficulty performing before

It looks with clearer eyes it doesn't speak with
forked tongue and no one
shrivels into a hard lump in its
presence and it now performs great
aerodynamic acrobatics of its own
inspired by such infectious positivity

Meanwhile the simple rebellious particle
has grown into an illuminated soul and is
ready to be let back into the main body
where with fresh face and no
resistance it now swims with the myriad
other particles in great troughs of
stars and oceans of interlocking beams
that is this world in which

actions that don't darken the atmosphere and
poison the ground for millennial generations
fly low over the glossy surfaces of things
touching them from time to time with their
miraculous touch and making the

real world come round again and
show itself in the most common mirror
as well as in mirror fragments and
mirrors cracked all the way through

with such force of beauty wedded to majesty

that all mirrors now happily become whole

9/28

34 UNDER THE SAME TREE

Tom sits under an apple tree and an
apple falls on his head and he
curses the universe and throws it
down the hill

Isaac sits under an apple tree and an
apple falls on his head and he
understands the universe
and walks into history

35 IN THE MIDDLE OF THE NIGHT

In the middle of the night I wake up with the
gnomes of expectation and the black cat of

inspiration arrayed around my bed
and the full moon of eradication and substitution

glowing like a gong over my head
and the half-open window of divine imagination

inviting what's outside to flow in and what's
inside to fly out

and the floorboards of firm foundation
under my feet should I actually try to

stand up in all this and totter forward
and the giraffes of spectral visitation glimpsed afar in the

far distance and I know they are angels
since no giraffes abide by here and I am a

realist

and the breathing walls of realism all around me
and the large night with all its galaxies right outside

and the unhesitant silence who has drawn in a
breath and held it all this time

for all eternity and yet maintained its
composure having expanded throughout time to

draw into its quiet ocean some of our
noisiest citizens such as Napoleon or Julius Caesar

or the ruthless victors and self-glorified tyrants who now lie
quiet under its cloth so pricked with stars

And all of these things by God's great grace
await a blessed outcome

before I even grip my pen
whose ink is like that held breath of

silence suddenly released across a page

And I only pray an angel's mouth directs it not my
own who spends too much time in idle chatter

and whose lips like two pillows press lightly together
expecting a sublime outburst at any moment to

force open their fleshy gates

10/1

36 BECAUSE THE SUBSTANTIAL AND THE INSUBSTANTIAL

Because the substantial and the insubstantial
flash back and forth through each other's dimensions with a
mesmerizing alacrity

so that swordfish about to penetrate a wall of water with their
pointy noses find themselves walls of water as well as
penetrating marauders

and air that holds clouds is just as
quickly the next world with its eternal
landscapes and billowing rose-shaped rainbows and
other basically indescribably splendorous
wonders

then like shirts turned inside-out they're
just as quickly a normal-looking street corner in say
some little Midwest town where all the
teenagers want to pierce their faces with
silver rings and run away

Except that their grim reality is actually
interpenetrated by an extra-molecular world of
marvels that would more than satisfy their
thirst for the supernatural if only they could
see them

As we ourselves fly apart in subatomic fluff then
just as quickly are reconstituted into
people passing each other in the street and
barely making eye contact or

lovers under the laundry inviting divine
whispers to fly down like yellow-breasted starlings to
circle their proclamations of love and
sing to the dazzling neon their passionate
eyes make in the dark

10/4

37 OH I'VE HAD IT WITH TALK

Oh I've had it with talk
and I've had it with silence

And I've had it with dogs who wear dress pants and
tell you what's on their mind when the
afternoon wind is rising

And I've had it with appearances and I've
had it with disappearances

And ships with volatile cargo crossing beneficent seas
in search of virgin Paradises to explore

I've had it with frivolous action and I've
had it up to here with sitting still

There's a caged bird of light the height of
Victoria Falls inside who wants to fly free

And I've had it with miniscule territories of love
when an ocean the color of green neon laps so
invitingly at our shores

And I've had it with long speeches
and short speeches where the heart sits well back behind the
front lines and shoots through the mouth

And I've had it with moving targets and I've
had it with inert ones who pretend otherwise

And I plan on doing something about it
and I'm doing it right now though I
may not know it or show it

A blade of blue silver across the horizon cutting
sky clear of earth and reversing them

Now that's better!

10/5

38 THE OLD WOMAN WHO LIVED IN A SHOE

There was an old woman who lived in a shoe
with zebra laces of aqua blue

There was a crooked man who walked a crooked mile
people would go out of their way to
avoid his crooked smile

Little Jack Horner sat in a corner
Afraid he'd have to speak to a foreigner

"Little Bo-Peep have you lost your sheep?"
"It's none of your business what hours I keep!"

Jack Sprat could eat no fat
so there was practically nothing where he sat

His wife could eat no lean
so don't be mean

39 THE KING AND THE SUNLIT COURTYARD

The king gazed long into the sunlit courtyard
until the courtyard was no more

The sunlit courtyard gazed long into the king
until the king was no more

The sycamore tree on the hill held up a chunk of the sky
to keep it from falling to pieces at the feet of the
lovers just over there
though they never even suspected they were in
any kind of danger since they'd
slipped into the perfect safety of each other's eyes
and nothing could distract them
even their own deaths
which took place exactly here
as the watercolor version of their embrace
was being hung at the Louvre and showed their
two enraptured faces and a long-suffering
sycamore tree seeming to hold up the
sky which in fact it was doing with no
word of complaint

The tree is still there
though the lovers have moved on
into the hillside beneath it
next to a very famous mole warren that
winds around the tree and on into
infinity

but just as infinity was turning to go after delivering a most
poignant farewell not heard since the
court of King Louis the XIV in the
glittering palace hung with its
infinity of mirrors

just as it was turning to go a voice called its name
and it stopped
turned back to the source of the voice and
pushed its hat way back on its head and said
"No one's ever done that before
I must be getting old"
and sat down in the shade to undo its
laces and run barefoot through the
clover

A pinwheel sat on a stem and turned its
lovely twisted blades until it became a
single point drawn in the air

I dove into that point and found you there
sitting by the side of the garden thinking

"Thinking what?" I asked myself
since all thinking seems to follow infinity
into the valley below where the
eternal river flows

"*Oh nothing really*" you replied
"*but the pictures hold for a moment before
shivering away forever never to return in
quite the same way*" said in a

rapid fluttering voice whose
intensity came and went

until a loud bellowing question from the
stones and trees was asked which
no one could answer

which is the way we like it

or like it or not
is the way it is

10/8

The way humans keep multiplying is quite touching

There are always new ones with bright faces walking
forward full of enthusiasm for the slightest things

wearing new fashions cutting their hair in new ways
just generally assuming the bright new world is theirs and
open to them for whatever adventure might present itself

including shopping in a suburban mall where I
am at the moment sitting on a hard wooden
bench with the plash of a continuous
fountain just behind me and soft music and
pleasant light and an endless coming and
going of these travelers who've come from a
dark womb where sperm and egg fused to be
a receptacle for spirit but not just any old

spirit rather a very particular
spirit both shared and not shared by everyone else
propelling them toward and repelling them away from
events momentous in their lives which I'm now

glimpsing for a tiny moment as they
go perhaps a few years later to buy fine jade in China and
drink tea in the Forbidden City or

sit on a small cushion in a mountain peak monastery
with wooden beads falling through their fingers with the

same watery regularity as the
fountain-waters at my back or the

echoey click-clack of footsteps across these
marble slabs from shop to shop as all

history holds its breath for a moment
to let these perfect preoccupied and slightly bewildered
divinely blessed people pass

10/9

41 SUBMERGED CITY

A submerged city underneath our eyelids
blue as a cobalt fog

An airplane rising above rain clouds suddenly blessed by a
rainbow horizon and the big bronze gong of the sun
sounding its Egyptian farewell on its way to the underworld

Doves in their dove cotes putting soft heads under wing-pits to sleep

All the dust in the world as it lands on everything after falling
incessantly from somewhere far away
perhaps as far away as the closest stars
and yet we go on with our bodily membranes
between the natural marvels of the colossal royal garden inside and the
so-called outside world where equally
miraculous things happen
under the tutelage of God's untiring gaze

We persist in quotidian uncertainty
even though the sun comes up again after its
subterranean voyage and paints
everything afresh with its luminous paintbox

invisible light like God's invisible breath

and the visible proof of His existence

that illuminates this intriguing shadow show

10/12

42 BRIGHT MORNING

Bright morning!
I see you tipping your golden baskets
in a nearby field
light pouring out like cobs of fresh-cut corn
spilling on the pathways

Slow music of cattle slow motion of time
even birds settle more slowly on branches
in no hurry to leap back into the air

A voice comes across the fields comes
like an ambling cloud
unmistakable unintelligible
yet proclaiming glory

Even the rankest grass blades
proclaiming glory this morning!

10/23

43 THROUGH ROSE-COLORED GLASSES

I

The spastic stops shaking for a moment and
looks the moon right in the face
the stars and distant heavens become suddenly
still

The paraplegic gazes at his limbs where his limbs used to be
and not only feels them but sees them as
real as tree branches birds land on and
do that mysterious wiping of their beaks on their
bark-like flesh

The blind who waft through my poems like a
theme open not their eyes but their
hearts as if their hearts have an eyelid that only needs to be
lifted to let light enter both in and out
for that is what our hearts are us blind ones
great ovals or rectangles or dimensionless
supra-geometrical areas for the
conducting of light as if

an ocean were a word that only needs to be
articulated in order for its deepest denizens to
come alive
as if the sky were a space-cranium open to ever-new ideas
and the stars were direct beams to shine on their
unique and particular brilliance

The sad one sees things worse than his despair
and breaks off a piece of his own and throws it
overboard

The suicide stops suddenly in mid-leap and leaps
back onto the precipice from which he'd
leapt and grows an armful of antlers each fitted with
gorgeously tinkling bells at their tips
with which he strides into town to entertain the
orphans just before naptime

Somehow these souls are singing with full voice through me now
as if a hospital corridor had turned inside-out in my
blood and every war-torn raped or otherwise
violated soul could be given back the
dimension stolen from it and could see the
possibility of Paradise on earth again through its
body of tears

Even death sitting there in a dark slouch at the
end of the hall looks up briefly with its
no face that fits all faces

and wipes a bit of strange moisture from its
sandpapery cheek
its eyes glistening in an unaccustomed way
and its imagination fills with a
vision of banquets on board Charon's death-barge
with souls raising glasses to the great
goodness of God in all circumstances
drinking down its heady wine with
no regrets and no complaints

as reality falls slowly over things again with its
tarnished pewter finish and its
pulsing flesh and bated breath

2

I've seen my dear friend's mother curled in her wrinkles like an embryo

her once glittering eyes gone flat and blank
her over-agile mouth wrenched down at one side now and slack
her active feet now stuck together as if lame out of feebleness
her often-wicked turn of mind now probably a large
windy place full of skittering dry leaves which never
find hard edges to fall against

thin cold and bony hands though the skin soft still
shrunken body largely useless now except as a
transformer of food from one end to the other
cared for by a bounteous black lady who's beginning to look like
James Brown a Jehovah's Witness with a heart bigger than
the moon but a body also held to this world by the
tenuous thread of dialysis

Where are those restless days and sad nights she passed so recently?
Where have the invisible children gone she used to
shoo out of the house in the middle of the night now that it seems
even her fantasy windows have clouded over
and the world's narrow compass of her body is helped from bed
and back into bed again?

"Your hands are so warm" I think she said
when I took her gnarled tree-branches into mine
though the recognition flickered out almost as
soon as it came

The stars and their slow circulations through a
shape of the universe we may never know

The arising and continual arising by God's command
of endless life as flakes of it fall away like shed skin
sloughed off by the friction of the forest floor as we
slide ever closer to the earth from which we've sprung

interpreting the heavenly signs written out on the blackest of skies
as personal notes to us from the
voice of love we can always hear in our hearts
if we just listen hard enough

as our body turns more and more to paper lit now by a low lamp
on which His words of love in careful watery script are written

3

The seashore has a foghorn that blows with a lion's moan

The palm tree has a cluster of berries whose oil burns an odorous red

The night opens its starry jacket to let fall burgled dreams

The day kicks a can down a desolate street in a downtrodden district
where the windows are blown out
and the doors are filled with rubble

The fat lady in the middle of the road's face
is more beautiful than a cluster of roses

The camel's eyes with long black lashes are those of a slave
handsomer than the king

The tail of the serpent of life disappears up ahead around
death's unforeseen bend

The smile on the circus acrobat about to leap into the air
turns into a trampoline of
white butterflies then into a deep cloud of blood

I've lived one life from its beginning to now
but dreamt of origins earlier than my own
in our horizontal human consciousness that knows no bounds
and whose endless deserts are lit by an alizarin sun

Whose eyes have these eyes encountered?

Into whose eyes has my heart descended in a single glance?

Our pupils are orbits greater than the transparent roads planets take
as they round their circles in space

and the pupils of our hearts are even greater still

in which the whole world continually turned inside-out
tunes and retunes its celestial song

10/25

44 THE WAY LIFE IS

We sink back up from the surfaces on which we float
to pursue today's very small paisley garland

45 THE PAGES ARE SILENT THE VOICE IS STILL

The pages are silent the voice is still

A great moose peers at us from between tall trees

The ocean rolls up into a ball then unrolls again and
flows

I haven't been there yet but I know it will be
wonderful

The reports are exquisite and the reporters without blemish

An opal the size of a turkey egg is brought in for our
inspection

Nothing turns out as we thought it would
or else the day would sag on its frame like a
dislodged canvas

Black horses don't gallop any faster than white
but a hair from the head of a saint has a
different tale to tell and smells of
rare roses

We can't move forward if we discard our oars in favor of
personal opinion

The doors of the truth don't swing open at our
command

The girl on the right in the picture with her
arm around the puppy dog may know more than the
grandfather with all the money in his pocket

If a tree bursts into flame right before your
eyes will all your doubts evaporate?

A ship in a bottle got in there somehow
but once inside it's only removal is the radical
smashing of glass

The escape into space is never easy
but the age demands it and our time is
limited

Love came in and sat among us but some of us
carried on talking

The heart resides where everyone wishes to go
but the guide remains silent until we lean close in
to listen

11/2

46 IN A DISTANT FOREST

In a distant forest you can just hear a flute
through the car horns
and it sounds like a speech from someone in anguish
a lament or now like a palpable heartbeat throb that
abandons a body in joy

Over the sounds of marching armies and aerial bombardment
the flute like a fakir's rope rises languidly or straight up
into the sky

Over the sounds of quarrels between couples who
fell into each other's eyes only a minute ago but then
took offense at a word or facial gesture
now their hearts erupt in broken prayers and embattled childhoods
a blue utopia dropped from a high wall
but their reconciliation is inevitable this time as well
in the flute song you can just make out whispering at the
edges of their momentary invectives

Ah the flute sound of a solitary flute player
in a forest nearby that begins to look like your own
his own her own the one unexasperating space of
openness between the thickets
where pure music can be heard
above even the deathbeds of peaceful holy ones
where it echoes monastically like celestial affirmation
but also above the derelict's death under newspapers

where sunlight beams filter through
fluttering branches to him in the helplessness of his squalor
showering a kind of strobe light onto the
innermost part of his crouched form

It can be heard in our vowels and consonants
cascades of ascending notes
already turning into the next valley

It can be heard as well in our silences
ruby light almost describing planetary motion

or certainly oceanic conversation from
our shore to a far shore

in a bridge of evanescent sound

11/3

47 SAD

Sad are they who've turned in their childhood
for an iron bar with wheels on it
that only goes uphill

Sad who've let the stinky dog in to the
glassed-in salon room that once smelled of lilacs
those who watched their reflection in the
rushing waterfall at the center of town
who now only stare in the full-length mirror on their
bedroom door

Who try to keep birds from flying over their roofs
when they were known for extra kindness to ants in the sandbox

Who won't look you in the eye nor respond to your
golden dimension with anything but the
cone-shaped aluminum one of their own

Sadness will overcome them one day as they
lock the outer door and listen to the
street children's voices over the fence
but they'll shrug it away and button their
top collar button or hunch their coat-shoulders
and continue walking straight ahead

They'll let bombs fall on
distant populations
and countries burn to a crisp beyond their visual gaze

having traded in their warm heartfelt bodies for those of
large insects with human-seeming faces with feelers and
front legs searching the air for contact
but finding none

Sad praying mantises are they
cocking their horizontal heads from side to side
very very sad

But their mates will
soon devour them!

11/5

48 THE DRINK

The beverage that lost Agamemnon drank
then faced his foe
the drink Doc Frankenstein gulped then
continued his dark cobbler's labors
the mug of light held to the lips of Prometheus on his rock
and his eyes opened and their pupils swam into focus

sip cooled and curdled in arctic snows
drawn from the same well where Joseph clung to the walls
until the Egyptian came

careful as rainwater on a bamboo trellis in Kyoto
that collects then spews from a spout into a black pool
shimmering in the moon

contained in a container for transport to the
destined recipient of such rare liquid refreshment
drop by drop siphoned from the mysterious reservoir of patience shared by
the Sphinx and Mona Lisa who mystify with nearly the
same smile looking out from the
same eyes across the same desolation

never left undrunk this potion of
urgency and illumination
never for a moment not drunk to the dregs somewhere on
earth by someone in the midst of
God's destined action
brought to bear by a mortal body

until the vessel is dry
filled again to the brim by the
Benevolent One
and drunk dry again in the midst of a
seeming whim

11/6

49 WAR

War bubbles up in the tea we're about to drink
between the alligators who live there
and the giant dragonflies who want to

A lumpy black form pulls itself up from the murky dregs

When the war is over a white cloth will fall from the sky
whose hem will be drenched in blood

I hope no one notices the heavy breathing in the corner
where the war began

I hope no one's fortunate enough to have won

11/9

50 THE EYE AND THE GARDEN

There's an eye the size of a pin in a
garden the size of the universe

and a garden the size of a pin
in an eye the size of the universe

and they're wrapped in a wind of no apparent size or
shape that has planets turning slowly inside its
amorphous sphere

and a voice wrapped around the whole of it so
sweet honey drips as if in Springtime from its
melodious words and swallows fly between their
floating honey-strands

and it is all as I've said though I'm not
here to say it

and a door opens as another door closes

and the voice on the other side *O Allah*

flows like an ocean around everything at once and
drowns it in magnitude and meaning

and holds it aloft to the light in its uplifting tides

11/13

51 THE HEART HAS REASON TO BELIEVE

Le coeur a ses raisons que la raison ne connaît point

— BLAISE PASCAL

The heart has reason to believe its tropical islands will bloom
giant scarlet palm trees whose
spraying spathes make golden pinwheels in a
bright blue sky

The heart has reason to believe the secret door to Allah's private
chamber opens here without benefit of lock
but whose key is that murmur on the lips of a lover
that reverberates through our bones to the
earth-bound bottoms of our toes

The heart has reason to believe in a sky whose opening eyelid
shows an eye that goes on and on into oracular oblivion
seeing every creation He's ever created from
time before time to time after time has expired

The heart has reason to believe it's riding a
team of wild white horses going at full gallop through all
the worlds and all the world's oceans at once
to run along a shore brought to life as we pass
whose faces open like white roses and whose
voices chime like silver bells

The heart has reason to believe the heart's God's residence
and we enter it with caution and with care
with courage and bravado for He's waiting there for our
entrance and His Face is already coming into focus in our sphere

The heart has reason to believe all this by the simple fact of being a heart
and not a steamboat or a plank of wood floating on black water
where moonlight cannot reach

And the spaces between the heart's beats are orbital dimensions
complete worlds come to birth in

and the beats themselves are His Name
as He names the worlds that come to birth

How can we not be delirious with love under these
perfect climactic conditions!

When He beckons us toward Him by the very
organ that keeps us alive

in the very chambers He's created for His voice
to echo and reecho in

calling us home!

11/15

52 TINY SCRATCHING NOISES

The train conductor pushes his hat back on his head and
holds a black bristle brush under his nose and proclaims
"I'm Karl Marx!"
Everyone laughs except the coal man who's
never read a book or looked at a
photograph with full comprehension

Aunt Ethel puts a doily from the table around her neck and
holds her head extremely high and sibilates
"I'm Queen Elizabeth the First!"
Everyone laughs except poor eighty-year old
Cousin Dahlia who's convinced
she's Queen Elizabeth the First
without a doily

Snopes Tweedle puts his arms down stiffly at his sides and
waddles forward shouting
*"I'm the first penguin Knut Rasmussen saw at the
Arctic Circle"* and
no one disputes him because they *all* think they're
penguins as well in the small and
docile coterie Snopes has gathered around him
in the institutional rotunda

as geese fly overhead slipping south from their summery personae
and identities glisten in early November sunlight
like cellophane behind whose vaguely shimmering surface
a deeper essence might be glimpsed emerging
into the sharper light of day

Although I am King Tut or Lucretia Borgia or
Alexander the Great dying on his shield after a
particularly debilitating debauch as historians say
or if he was actually a prophet
because of some virus sent his way by Gabriel or another potent
angel to fell him as his successes on earth became
too overwhelming for everyone
even for him

"I am" at all is a dodgy proposition
and as soon as we *"find ourselves"* which will most
probably take a lifetime

our lifetime's measure of sand has nearly essentially
run out and the eye of light that pierces through masks and
masquerades may dawn with angelic comprehension

But if we just see now that transparency is the key and
being somebody was a pretty sorry project in the
first place since *"being"* and *"somebody"* don't really even
belong to us just as *"belong"* itself also really doesn't either

He Who Is alone is

He Who Is alone will be

He Who Is alone was

He who Is is enough for all

None are but He alone

Then the luminous pink conch shell on the beach holds the
entire ocean in its iridescent coil inward to
silence

and the mouse family scurrying between walls
holds generic encyclopedias of future mouse generations
nearly simultaneous with the present one so
prolific are they

and the night hits its gong of darkness irradiated by the
full moon and then hits the gong of the
full moon with its own light to become
resonatingly silent

and the heart too becomes silent

and silence itself becomes silent at last
before blossoming out again into

tiny scratching noises

11/21

53 A THOUSAND STAMPEDING ELEPHANT HOOVES

A thousand stampeding elephant hooves
making the earth their drum with their
cosmic beat reaching earth's molten core
the energy dissolving in fiery thick atomic soup blast

The beat of a trillion gnat wings soda crackering
above an abyss and catching sun rays so it
looks like the air's been slivered into trillions of
twinkling slivers spelling out some Morse Code no
mortal can decipher though intelligent angels might understand

One second's worth of the breaths of everyone on earth
the moment caught as our breaths enter their apogee and release
exhaling the subtlest delicate tidal wave of fineness that
wavers a frail plant blade somewhere perhaps or
may make a cloud move a fraction and
the climate change from fair to foul or from foul to fair

Eyeblinks flickering with the same stampeding energy though a
bit more quietly than those stampeding elephant hooves of the
first stanza more like the gnat wings of the second
and the gossamer thought of the Creator of all this as it
shimmers in the mind's heart or the heart's mind
like a distant star made suddenly near
or like a near-most phenomena taking place in an
evanescent dazzle in unending darkness

His near brooding hovering over us
His dear concern for each breath of us each lid-beat heart-
throb of each tiniest one of us from
first to last with no clear hierarchy
since the worm wriggles to its own safety in the mud
and the fly buzzes across a pond at daybreak with the
same brilliant aplomb as a commuter intent on
making it safely across the bridge into New Jersey on a
Monday or Tuesday and those

elephant hooves making their definite music somewhere
behind us and the beat of starlight making its
metronomic pulse with the same rhythmic regularity
somewhere above us

11/23

54 ORPHEUS' HEAD

I

Orpheus' head may float down the river
cut like egg-slices by the strings of his lyre
making his voice though single an ethereal chord
that still attracts beasts both
four-footed and two-footed mammal and
insect as gorgeous jewel-like dragonflies land on his
eyelids and flies buzz their iridescent
crowns around his live poetic brow

Ah the mist over the dark river twines with the twang of his
words underscored by his lyre-song's melodious rising
and though workers on the banks
threshing wheat and gathering corn don't
notice this glowing blue magnificence passing by them
his red tongue never stops with its praises to God and its
nonsense syllables *alook alook garganto babba so*
long are my sorrows so blue are my skies
though my body is light-headed now and my
head disembodied yet nothing veils me from
perfection seen from below as I float downstream to a
music so utterly otherworldly it has
nothing of the human in it only

space and closed eyelids a vision of totality
seen from inside this cranial coliseum afloat on
earth's surface under moonlight and
sunlight under pain and release from pain
making its narrow watery way
to God's open sea

2

A stag stopped statuesquely in its tracks to listen

A raccoon stopped pillaging and stood on its
bandito's hind legs for a full minute enthralled

A mountain lion slunk to a stop and actually purred

Even ants in continual procession lined up
somewhere en route from
somewhere on their way to somewhere and
caught their breath as it were feelers twitching
listening to Orpheus' song

Capable of sustaining a falling autumn leaf for a
full minute twisting in space
or a snowflake stalled on its refrigerated
trajectory meltdown earthward

Even amoebas might slow down to his circadian rhythms and
circle round each other in a curious primordial polka
since his song emptied of himself cut in two
tickles ivories yet unknown and cracks glasses yet unground
elemental songster God's appointed larynx in physical manifestation
lurching disembodiedly bloody-necked from the
unseen into our sphere

Such crooning as it passes land masses freeze-frames
various warm-blooded and cold-blooded
creatures like snakes and
newts who bounce their beady-eyed heads to its
live rhythms for a second before devouring flies

Orpheus descending! Making lasting impressions on even
tree bark and rocks
signature veinwork imbedded in the very nature of our
most mortal enterprise

Blue pewter blond rainbow elixir of silence
singer of death-song
star envisioner long after the mortal body's gone!

3

Sympathetic strings resound under your sobs
which are not sobs
your laments which are a clearing of the throat for

entrance into the next world
your unearthly chant that sounds like a
dozen shamans gone deliriously into trance

Somehow even the edges of heaven have contracted a
little like a concertina emitting a few
wheezy notes to accompany your sound

Flakes of an uncertain brilliance fall through the air
cranes fly through the flake-streams like shuttles through a
loom to weave the sky

Like a thimble now your head flows downriver to
the water-source from which it sprang
ocean of origin and sounded chord of incessant tremors
in the sunset's gong

Head blithely singing unto light no matter what

unheard or unlistened to except by the
silent choirs of the night

Each note of your song a perfectly pitched pearl
gleaming in starlight

11/28-12/1

55 ECSTATIC DANCING

After an hour and a half of ecstatic dancing

After fifteen minutes of ecstatic dancing

After twenty-five and a half minutes of ecstatic dancing

After just ten minutes of ecstatic dancing

After being held for just one minute to the central cyclotron of
ecstatic dancing

After being run down by stampeding horses of ecstatic dancing and
clutching tight to their glistening manes

After disappearing for long periods of time in the ramshackle
shack flying apart in ecstatic dancing

After one solid minute under the waterfall of ecstatic dancing

After sighting land afar off under pink clouds and
green sunlight in the brilliant golden sky of ecstatic dancing

After concluding then deconcluding in the
heightened inconclusive argument of the self shivered down to its
essential non-existence in the super reality of ecstatic dancing

After crickets and songbirds and every howling animal on earth
join together in the untouched Paradise of ecstatic dancing

After dreaming and waking up and then waking up
in the dream of being awake forever in ecstatic dancing

After plucking the ripe fruit and digesting it completely in just one
delicious moment of ecstatic dancing

After being transformed from a butterfly into a
freight train and from a freight train into a
redwood forest and from a redwood forest into a
snowy mountain range of weeping willows in the
moonlight and from that snowy mountain range of weeping willows
into pure moonlight itself in ecstatic dancing

After one breath of Allah taken and received and given out into the
world again in just one unbated breath of ecstatic dancing

And after the endlessness of this poem that will
continue long after it's finished in the endlessly
energized eternity of ecstatic dancing

After ecstatic dancing is done and begun again
and we enter into its core as we
were at the first and will be at the last again deathless and
breathless in ecstatic dancing

After just one second of ecstatic dancing

After God's blessed message excites us again
to ecstatic dancing

12/3

56 THE STUPENDOUSNESS OF PERCEPTION

Everything falls meticulously into place
It can't do otherwise

There's no room for error

The water of light overflows everywhere

Seek a door and a wall will arise
Seek a wall and a door lets you enter His Garden

In paradox is the mainspring that keeps the clock ticking

In the Garden is a lone peacock who ignites into a phoenix
briefly lighting up the sky

In our love for it all is His generous Hand made manifest
In the light of our eye is the answer to its earlier tears

There's no betrayal in the white signpost
that turns us back into the *palacio* of our self

after light has touched the main beam
after the dogs have all turned into solemn doormen in blue uniforms

awaiting the high-pitched whistle
that will call them all home

12/9

57 PARISIAN SOJOURN

I

Although we're in Paris
in a lovely little cubbyhole hotel in Montmartre
where the lift is just big enough for one
person at a time unless you happen to be a
few dozen yardsticks on legs
I wonder exactly what Paris we're in?

Are we in the Paris of wildly Art Nouveau black iron bridges over
swans frozen in ice rivers pecking their breasts to
feed their young motherly blood drops?

Are we in the Paris of bohemian rooftop garrets where
beauty is being driven to excess until in a convulsive paroxysm
it becomes actually a beatified ascetic in ashen overcoat above a
brazier of flames who proclaims the death of all but the
anthropomorphized railroad train eating the
intimate details of its passengers' private lives?

Or raindrops on Paris rooftops each one a
crystal ball with silver-flake snowfall inside showing forth yet another
Utopian city of rock crystal and radically idealized affirmation?

The people out this rainy night along the
cobblestone boulevards looked normal enough
but I know they carry secrets from underground resistance groups
and strategies for renewed attacks against the bourgeoisie for which they are
in fact the best representatives

Arthur Rimbaud's icy violet countenance hardened by a death he
so accurately predicted
stares out of each face here with the key to this
sideshow which still remains: *Charity!*

The reversal of everything we see

and somehow faith in the most
gorgeous truths we've ever known

2

The first night in Montmartre I had a
long and peculiar dream that involved a very
large and charismatic man whose
presence had a special resonance and whose
actions were those of a savior

He somehow figured in a battle of good and
evil with troops of people against him and a
vulnerable band of folk
in a giant tank of dark green water or perhaps in the
ocean

and at a certain moment it became clear that
if he was decapitated his people would suddenly
rally and overcome their enemies but also

his martyrdom would assure them victory

So he dove down into the water and
his head came off

The atmosphere shifted at once and in the
chaos good was prevailing
and he emerged headless with bloody neck but still
living holding a girl across his huge arms whom he
carried onto dry land and into her
chamber this giant headless man with
water dripping from his back carrying a
girl dressed in diaphanous white to safety

I remembered the dream in the morning
and then came across lines in the
guidebook for Montmartre that one theory of the origin of the
Mount of Martyrs name commemorates
the martyrdom of St. Denis patron saint of Paris
who was beheaded on this highest hill in Paris in the 1600s
and buried there
but distressed at the location of his burial he
himself carried his head in his arms and
walked across Paris to his
preferred final resting place

3

Only in Paris could a quiz-show question on TV be
"How many sets of wings on the Seraphim?"

Or the twinkly little old lady I talked to coming down the
steps from the Sacre Coeur cathedral say that
writers and poets bring people new
perceptions and visions of life as she repulsed an
African bracelet salesman by saying *"Nyet!"* and we
descended the stairs to the sounds of an
ancient carousel tall and light-studded and calliope-jaunty in the
Montmartre dusk

In the Salvador Dali museum with its
black walls and his deep dramatic voice over the
PA system rolling his "r's" extravagantly
among the phantasmagoric bronzes and splatter-delicate lithographs
of bearded anchorites hobbling out of blotch red cloud or
squirming lovers holding radiant heads in a state of
Catholic ecstasy on the back of a cloud horse

The Eiffel Tower has turned to gold from our faraway window
like the Seraphim with their three sets of wings
(the correct answer)
presiding over Paris

And various angels with various wings float in the
fog blowing various Renaissance trumpets
as buses and Pugeots grind along the streets down below
and Rilke says *"So this is where people come to live –
I would have thought it is a city to die in"*

While Nijinsky whom I'll visit tomorrow God willing in the
Montmartre cemetery of the Sacred Heart
leaps higher in the air than ever in his grave

and actually stays there

4

Nijinsky! What angels are you teaching new
ways to fly what irrepressibly avant-garde
angels are escorting you with their
new ways of wing-flow and three sets of
wingbeats making radiant arcs in delicious four dimensional
incandescent sweeps through the air you so
easily leap through as if

acrobatics had never even needed to be invented
though of course among spiritualized molecules as you are also a
spiritualized molecular body now with a soul on the
outside instead of on the inside as it is in our
bodily mortal sojourn

Your avenues of invention have opened infinitely wider
and the pink-blue horizon as in a painting by Fragonard
splashing more obviously as you stamp your ethereal
feet now perhaps and penetrate time and space in a way
you never could for any real length of time on earth

Are lines of angels with their toes turned in
as in the *Sacre de Printemps* moving among
silver-tinted clouds?

Are spirals of wing-flutters turning inward to
one rhythm while tetrahedral spherical shapes spiral outward again
to another? For flames to ignite are a
billion or so angels in the compact space of a
dot suddenly blooming like an extravagant
chrysanthemum of staggering brightness?

Your strange almost simian face lit by God's own
intimate Light your exclamations of godly
Halajian identity making perfect sense now
in the only dimension it ever made sense in
where His voice and our actions His commands and
our obedience His light and our bedazzled
shadows are explosively and serenely one?

Ah Vaslav I visited your sweet tomb in
Montmartre today its green iron statue of you sitting in the
poignant pose of *Petrouchka* surrounded I was so
happy to notice by flowers and plants in the
gray Parisian drizzle and someone had put a
red rose in your hand as you had a
red rose in your teeth when you leapt sideways through the
famous window in the *Spectre de la Rose* ballet
staying aloft seemingly forever as I prayed there you're
staying aloft now for all eternity among your most
noble companions

even the still photo images of you giving us inspirations of
eternal delight

5

for Odelon Redon and Gustave Moreau

A blind man suddenly has no mouth and
becomes a saint

A dog laps milk with its wet tongue and becomes a centaur
with great golden wings

A bumblebee loses its black stripes and looks at
itself in a blue lake and sees that it has the
face of a prophet whose face is never
graphically represented to mankind

The Four Horses of the Apocalypse chomp grass nonchalantly by the
side of a burning road because in
spite of the encroaching disaster a few people sing songs and
trust God's Mercy and hold hands in a
circle and refuse to be afraid

I've seen a dragon's tail lift its delicate barbs above our heads
in the most inconspicuous places
and yet we continue our conversations about nearly nothing at all
as if nearly nothing at all is about to take place
and nothing will change

A clown in Chinese face-paint turns a
somersault on top of a grizzly bear's head

on a motorcycle in a circle spotlit the brightest white
at the far end of an alleyway in some forgotten Mongolian city
and the two hundred people are amazed beyond belief
and go home to their yurts and dream of a Paradise of
bright colors cool waters and green valleys
delicious grapes and cantaloupes on trays brought by
servants whose eyes are like glorious sunrises chasing away
every darkness known to man until morning

An ant picks up a leaf and finds the wisdom of
Prometheus written on its veins and faints dead away

A spider weaves its web between the bedpost of a king and a
poor man's hovel and catches red creatures with wings no one's
ever seen before

The spider of justice the spider of delight

The spider of God's voice calling each of us to Him
in the night

6

When I got on the crowded Metro there was one
double seat empty because a woman was sitting in
one of them everyone seemed to be avoiding and when I
glanced at her so did I

She had long ratty black hair with a few gray
streaks in it and was leaning forward erect
rubbing her forehead

I moved to the side next to it and
decided to sit on the vacant seat across from her
anyway since she at least didn't seem dangerous she wasn't
mumbling or raving she was just *Les Miserables*
tragic

She had a loose knit gray sweater on and long
black skirt and a broken gray
leatherette bag she had plonked down on
the seat next to her

Her forehead had bloody scabs she seemed to be
picking with dirty fingernails and she
reeked that reek of sleeping in her
clothes and radically needing a bath

But her face was somehow elegant
almost masculine
black eyes that looked around but didn't seem to look at
anything but their own blackness
a long aquiline nose and lips pursed tight so
used to suppressing complaint or perhaps to
loudly proclaiming it in her agonies of solitude because she
seemed in an agony of solitude even here on the
crowded Metro

having effectively held everyone around her at
bay by her stench and her reaching into her
sweater endlessly to scratch and search the empty air
with her blank black eyes for some relief

I wondered to myself if I could manage to
give her some money
so reached into my pocket under my overcoat and took out
my coin purse and counted out five Euros
and imagined various scenarios of putting out my
hand just before getting off so she wouldn't have to
thank me for it or elaborately reject it or
even in one violent scenario suddenly break her
purse-lipped silence and scream obscenities at me for
daring to give her charity
throwing the coins at me in this crowded train car

But finally before nearing my stop by one or two
stops I asked her if she would accept some
money from me and her face suddenly
focused on mine for a moment in silence so I
added *"to get something to eat"*
and she said simply but somehow nobly
"I've already had breakfast"

and just as quickly went back to her sad preoccupations
though when I got up to leave and said
"au revoir" she faintly and tragically
smiled at me and there was a small

but a very small
understanding between us

7

The Sphinx winks!
I mean there it is on its rock ledge enigmatically
staring down having posed the great question and also having
the answer to it up its feline sleeve and the
astonished acolyte puzzling between one
answer and another while also contemplating the
skulls and bones of earlier contestants whose
pale answers proved so totally inadequate
trembling at the thought of that lion-bodied human-visaged
Sphinx gnawing down on his head bone and even really
wondering how he had gotten into this predicament in the first place
his whole life up to this point now so dependent on his
correct answer to this enigmatic question
"How many pairs of wings do the Seraphim have?"

When all of a sudden

the Sphinx winks!

Does this quiz beast know it's all a joke? Or

dandles the sad answerer between two punishing abysses
then laughs right in his face?

I mean
here we are with all our poor knowledge and worse all our
pretences at knowing anything at all in fact

Here we are face to face with the abyss itself
centuries of quests and hanging questions dangling behind us

We're looking right into the inscrutable eyes of the
questioner *The Great Questioner* Whose Power lies in
putting us on the spot we'd hoped never to be put on

And the face so solemn and stentorian so placid and implacable

The Sphinx winks!

So many have fallen at this moment

So many have dropped their guard thinking in fact it's
really not all that important after all and we'll soon be
adjourning for a hot dinner or a straight whiskey
all taboos having miraculously been lifted

It's OK after all to worship the idols all around us it's
just fine to cheat on all our promises or
slide by with half-truths and mediocre knowledges
and we're very close to thinking we can
get away with winking right back at the
Sphinx say
even maybe giving it a nudge with our
elbow to show we've been in on the
joke all along

When suddenly the Sphinx stops winking in
mid-wink in fact and we see now
a Sphinx with slitted eyes looking at us
those brilliant emeralds beaming like lasers

right through to our hearts

and all the world but this precarious ledge we're on
falling entirely away

So that it's just Sphinx-face and our face
eye-to-eye and face-to-face and no wink for miles but the
question boring through us now and not the
quiz-show question whose answer was *"Three!"*

Not so easy

Not so fast

But the total answer of our lives held in suspension here
among silver clouds

and the wing-beats of eagles

8

"The difference between visions and dreams" he said
and his head went off in a different direction

"The difference between visions and dreams" he explained
and lines of tiny seahorses galloped in the air

"The difference between visions and dreams" he continued
and gold palm trees shot up out of nowhere

Until a door opened flooded with a different light than
four walls and a window could tolerate

Horse faces now bigger than canyons horse eyes bigger than
the moon and wilder

Oceans of tumultuous red banners and boats of human bones

"The difference lies in which direction they go in"
he tried to elucidate

as photo-clear vistas bathed in the light of God's Face
sprang into view that caught our hearts in a
brilliant effulgence

A tiny speck on the horizon
that grew into a world

whose giraffes all had wings
and whose rivers all sang in unison

9

The fat cat Coffee greets us crying when we get home after
two weeks away

The black cat Raven slinks off and hides not sure or
complicated and hurt playing hard to get

Coffee sniffs the suitcases and runs her claws down the
hemp fabric side and jumps on the shirts

Raven's under our round living room table now still unconvinced

Coffee takes it all in stride and soon's curled up on her favorite chair

I reach under the table and scratch Raven's chin after she sniffs my hand

Coffee falls asleep occasionally waking up to look at us and meow

Raven starts purring at last and purrs
for the next three hours straight

Coffee is definitely happy to see us she walks around as
usual eats her kibble drinks sleeps wakes up meows

Raven purrs like a dynamo
and leans into her head-scratching with all her black soul

Coffee is upstairs now because I just heard her crack a kibble bit

Raven's at the foot of my bed in the morning purring like a bicycle with playing cards in its spokes

12/16-12/24

58 SWEET OBLITERATIONS OF WONDER

Allah is not ashamed to make an example of a gnat
Or of an even smaller thing

— QUR'AN (2/26)

O You Who gives the snail his built-in spiral taxicab
always on his back as he
oozes to his next destination

Who lets the fruit fly nap for a spell
during its thirty-seven hour lifetime
though to it it's life itself as it
wakes refreshed to continue
annoying the outdoor street venders

You who rolls the dice of seasonal weather
showing one moment sunlight the
next all laced together with a fine slant
rain or a fog so thick greedy
drivers pile up on speedfreak highways delirious

O most Gracious You Who somehow makes a
rhino attractive to another rhino or else
we'd have no rhinos at all blinking nearsightedly as
those white birds oblivious to rhino emotions of any kind
use their backs for island landing strips
preening their feathers or just standing still

O You Whose infinitely detailed considerations are so amply
evident in the creation and to Whom I'm so
utterly grateful even I must admit when I
forget to be so

Intimate and Ultimate Punctuator of all our
sentences and clauses with every unavoidable
comma or hyphen semi-colon or exclamation point in place
so that our destinies read perfectly in the
silence of reality or in its dramatic reading
to the echoing canyons with their heavenly buttes acting like
pinball obstacles for the sound as it tilts its
way to its goal its silver ball
shining like a planet

O God Who remains elusive even as Your
clues are as manifest in such abundance
as those of a criminal who desperately wants to get caught
You leaving such signs behind as the sociableness of ants and bees
the ingenuity of elephants and giraffes bridge builders and plumbers
the perfection of cherry blossom buds that the Japanese
make pilgrimages out of
Tokyo to see to this day not even necessarily calling them
signs of Your workmanship
though each delicately nuanced pink edge or white center
points elegantly in Your direction

O God whose sudden and slow-in-coming
blessings have poured onto me like the
excited words of a racehorse announcer as the
wildly named gallopers come round the last bend to the finish line
breathing flame

and these pale metaphors are all I have to
offer in return though they don't even begin to
properly fathom Your mysteries or Your Majesty

Perhaps the astrophysicist does it better in his
logbooks of meticulous data or the heart surgeon as he
successfully sews one capillary onto another and the
tiny bloodstream trickles from old to new
to the patient's unconscious well being

I sit now in my wintry bed under a giant red
duvet dreaming of Your endless variants of Grace on us
to the *point final* of mute astonishment

The squirrel who scuttles across on a telephone wire
with no bar or umbrella

The Prophet who puts his hand in a water jug and the water
flows so copiously a giant multitude drinks from it

I can't formulate enough instances of perfection to
properly recognize Yours
and I'm only trying to reinforce some kind of

itemization of the obvious to slick away the
sleep from my own eyes for a moment in this chilly December night
this wholly inadequate blurt of thankful praise
for the Giver of all gifts in such
intricate detail and overpowering beauty that the
subtlety of Your signature on all things
makes them even more signed masterpieces of Your
infinite Presence

and the tactile blessings that fall like a
fine mist each of us feels
our hands to our cheeks our mouths agape
inspire in our hearts again
such sweet obliterations of wonder

                                    12/26

59 WHAT IS A POEM?

"What is a poem
and how should we react to it"

I always hear hooves or something very like hooves
drumming towards me at the inception of a
poem or when a poem's about to be
read that's more than quotidian platitudes

A railroad train heading towards us
that's caught roses on its cow-catcher

A drink whose strands of interweaving bouquet
precede it

A moonless night where there's a
sudden illumination in the trees

A man stands up with no face and starts
speaking and slowly a face appears
moving lips first
then gradually and elaborately the
rest of his features
ending with real eyes looking at us

girls crushing grapes upriver so that the
waters that reach us are dyed blue

and when we hear a poem that's full of
migrating birds or the
crackle of flames or a solitary harpist

and our hands don't get clammy
or something more than looking at a
calendar picture occurs

and we can see trout leaping through the waterfall

we can either keep the secret or spill it
use its light to cross the reconnaissance map or lose it

give the poet masses of money and hot soup
or watch him go accompanied by his
favorite giraffe until the
next one comes along

People have been known to wake from the
dead at a great poem
regaining mortal composure from their
condition of bones

or leap through adolescence altogether as if through a
flaming hoop
and appear with the lantern of Diogenes on a
dark street in a foreign city late at night
speaking the language

12/28

60 THE DEAD YOUNG GIRL SUPINE

The dead young girl supine
floated out of the room and across to the
harbor where she stood upright in the
air and boarded a freighter for Tahiti

If that seems improbable
three small ponies clambered onto each other's
backs in imitation of the Trojan Horse whose
pictures they saw one day torn from a book and
blown into their pasture
and somehow God wanted them to melt together into
one big horse who stood majestic and white the next
morning to the astonishment of their owner

Such tall tales should be easy to fabricate out of
whole cloth

Such as the day the Chinese noodle inventor actually
thought to chop it into lengths instead of
trying to cook and serve one continuous
noodle back somewhere in the Neolithic
with a sharp rock and the utter and total
disapproval of his wife and other conservative
traditionalists

Or the first to go up in a gas balloon having somehow
inflated his shirt by mistake
lifting him bodily off the earth and taking him above the
tall dark cypresses onto the estate of his future
partner and backer in the innovative and lucrative
international ballooning business

The fact that one thing flows into the next or that
nothing holds onto its fixed identity forever
helps in this mortal earthly sphere

The only things that remain after all being
The Divine Names in their rotation and mobilization
one after another or one superimposed within
the other with either flashing inner lights or
a dull somber radiant glow like burnished amber
each moment presenting us a new face and another facet of
the Unified Singularity of Reality
as if seen through rose-colored glasses

The Goldfish who wanted to be king and
outgrew its bowl in a single splash

The limousine driver who wanted only to be
an Olympic swimmer in those interplanetary goggles
free of wide turning maneuvers and the need for
huge parking spaces

Or the gnat the lowly gnat who was
finally happiest being just that

Everything in its closeup detail
just perfect as it is for the perfectly

satisfied gnat after all

just like that

12/31

61 RABBITS OUT OF HATS

Rabbits out of hats locomotives out of tunnels
moose antlers that negotiate sparse Canadian woods
goldfish leaping through rainbows
death and its aftermath death and its furry glove thrown so
carelessly onto the surface of a silver lake where it
floats for a full ten minutes before sinking into the dark
all these emergences into our frail realities
wet noses first asking us to chuck them behind the ears with
excessive affection

And we do somehow though the blizzard nearly blind us or the
fire nearly gut us as well as the doll warehouse whose
paint cans explode a
mile into the air with extravagantly colorful fireworks

One figure arrives in peacock feather mask with real eyes
while another figure in long strips of black cloth
exits with little pomp through a door in
space we hadn't noticed existed

leaving us in this room of boisterous crowds and
puzzled merchants having to choose between a
red ribbon and a green silk cord
for tying all our loose ends together

Allah be merciful as You so actually are
on the overlooked details and the things we
think up to derail us

Put us on our feet again for the
twelfth time after falling down then the
thirteenth time then the fourteenth time and so on until forever
when our gravity feet will have been exchanged for
wingéd shoes or no feet at all to speak of
to lead us into the forbidden territories of our torrid zones

and we'll ride free to meet You on Your own terms at last
with the perfection You expect and had created in us
in the first place until You break our porcelain shell

and flashes of perfect sunlight stream out all around us
into the nooks and crannies of the world
exposing to Your mercy even the
most microscopic of entities

even the shyest mouse huddled among his shivering
brothers and sisters

in the darkest of corners

1/7

62 WE CLIMB ON THE PLOW

The cut worm forgives the plow
— WILLIAM BLAKE

We climb on the plow and start
threshing the corn that grows uphill

The sun is beating down
and our body groans under this monumental labor

Golden tassels golden leaves golden stalks
rotation of sharp knife-edges to make the
fresh harvest

If we were of the vegetable kingdom we might hear the
corn scream and think it was murder

The day is long and the harvesting successful
and among the luscious ears gleam diamonds

I heard this song from the threshers in the fields
and in the distance a coyote yowl:

Saint Everyone go to the Creator and bow
Saint Everyone thank Him for this yield

Our life gutters to a lowering flame
but today we know He has smiled

Blackbirds fly in formation across the sun
but when they're gone the sun's bright as a shield

Love plants the garden our blades of love cut down
May love ignite our hearts and make them mild

And may the love that is in the strength of our arms
be also in the scythes we're meant to wield

1/13

63 ON THIS SIDE FIELDS ARE GRAY

On this side fields are gray
On that side fields stretch away into sparkling green

On this side we grow old and die
On that side a flock of snowy egrets flies from our hearts
into eternal sunrise

On this side our faces crack and their mercurial expressions wrinkle
On that side a light in our eyes lights up room after room of
bright children laughing

On this side a lone black horse clops down cobblestone alleyways
On that side distance to the ground is in
direct proportion to a general buoyancy and exhilaration

On this side even our best intentions sometimes fall by their own weight
On that side each wall has a glass door that opens inward

On this side what we're served soon grows cold
On that side a stream rushes by carrying
every succulence there for the plucking

On this side these words must face their endless inadequacy
On that side silence eloquently outlines each pine needle leaf and barely
visible breath with its intricate lexicon

On this side we wear rose-colored glasses to see light
On that side a rose of light grows in the splendor of its perfection
through the transparency of everything

1/15

ABOUT THE AUTHOR

Born in 1940 in Oakland, California, Daniel Abdal-Hayy Moore's first book of poems, *Dawn Visions*, was published by Lawrence Ferlinghetti of City Lights Books, San Francisco, in 1964, and the second in 1972, *Burnt Heart/Ode to the War Dead*. He created and directed *The Floating Lotus Magic Opera Company* in Berkeley, California in the late 60s, and presented two major productions, *The Walls Are Running Blood*, and *Bliss Apocalypse*. He became a Sufi Muslim in 1970, performed the Hajj in 1972, and has lived and traveled throughout Morocco, Spain, Algeria and Nigeria, landing in California and publishing *The Desert is the Only Way Out*, and *Chronicles of Akhira* in the early 80s (Zilzal Press). Residing in Philadelphia since 1990, in 1996 he published *The Ramadan Sonnets* (Jusoor/City Lights), and in 2002, *The Blind Beekeeper* (Jusoor/Syracuse University Press). He has been the major editor for a number of works, including *The Burdah* of Shaykh Busiri, translated by Shaykh Hamza Yusuf, and the poetry of Palestinian poet, Mahmoud Darwish, translated by Munir Akash. He is also widely published on the worldwide web: *The American Muslim* and *DeenPort,* among others. His current 21st century website is at: www.danielmoorepoetry.com, and his poetry blog at: http://ecstaticxchange.wordpress.com. *The Ecstatic Exchange Series* is bringing out the extensive body of his poetry in book form (complete list on page 2).

Dawn Visions (published by City Lights, 1964)
Burnt Heart/Ode to the War Dead (published by City Lights, 1972)
This Body of Black Light Gone Through the Diamond (printed by Fred
    Stone, Cambridge, Mass, 1965)
On The Streets at Night Alone (1965?)
All Hail the Surgical Lamp (1967)
States of Amazement (1970)

Abdallah Jones and the Disappearing-Dust Caper (published by The Ecstatic
    Exchange/Crescent Series, 2006)
The Chronicles of Akhira (1981) (published by Zilzal Press with Typoglyphs by Karl
    Kempton, 1986)
Mouloud (1984) (A Zilzal Press chapbook, 1995)
Man is the Crown of Creation (1984)
The Look of the Lion (The Parabolas of Sight) (1984)
The Desert is the Only Way Out (completed 4/21/84) (Zilzal Press chapbook, 1985)
Atomic Dance (1984) (am here books, 1988)
Outlandish Tales (1984)
Awake as Never Before (12/26/84) (Zilzal Press chapbook, 1993)
Glorious Intervals (1/1/85) (Zilzal Press chapbook, ?)
Long Days on Earth/Book I (1/28 – 8/30/85)
Long Days on Earth/Book II (Hayy Ibn Yaqzan)
Long Days on Earth/Book III (1/22/86)
Long Days on Earth/Book IV (1986)
The Ramadan Sonnets (Long Days on Earth/Book V) (5/9 – 6/11/86) (Published by
    Jusoor/City Lights Books, 1996) (Republished as Ramadan Sonnets by The
    Ecstatic Exchange, 2005)
Long Days on Earth/Book VI (6-8/30/86)
Holograms (9/4/86 – 3/26/87)
History of the World (The Epic of Man's Survival) (4/7 – 6/18/87)
Exploratory Odes (6/25 – 10/18/87)
The Man at the End of the World (11/11 – 12/10/87)
The Perfect Orchestra (3/30 – 7/25/88)
Fed from Underground Springs (7/30 – 11/23/88)
Ideas of the Heart (11/27/88 – 5/5/89)
New Poems (scattered poems, out of series, from 3/24 – 8/9/89)
Facing Mecca (5/16 – 11/11/89)
A Maddening Disregard for the Passage of Time (11/17/89 – 5/20/90)
The Heart Falls in Love with Visions of Perfection (6/15/90 – 6/2/91)
Like When You Wave at a Train and the Train Hoots Back at You (Farid's Book)
    (6/11 – 7/26/91)
Orpheus Meets Morpheus (8/1/91– 3/14/92)

The Puzzle (3/21/92 – 8/17/93)
The Greater Vehicle (10/17/93 – 4/30/94)
A Hundred Little 3-D Pictures (5/14/94 – 9/11/95)
The Angel Broadcast (9/29 – 12/17/95)
Mecca/Medina Time-Warp (12/19/95 – 1/6/96) (Published as a Zilzal Press
    chapbook, 1996)
Miracle Songs for the Millennium (1/20 – 10/16/96)
The Blind Beekeeper (11/15/96 – 5/30/97) (Published 2002 by Jusoor/Syracuse
    University Press)
Chants for the Beauty Feast (6/3 – 10/28/97)
Open Doors (10/29/97 – 5/23/98)
Salt Prayers (5/29 – 10/24/98) (Published by The Ecstatic Exchange, 2005)
Some (10/25/98 – 4/25/99)
Flight to Egypt (5/1 – 5/16/99)
I Imagine a Lion (5/21 – 11/15/99)(Published by The Ecstatic Exchange, 2006)
Millennial Prognostications (11/25/99 – 2/2/2000)
The Book of Infinite Beauty (2/4 – 10/8/2000)
Blood Songs (10/9/2000 – 4/3/2001)
The Music Space (4/10 – 9/16/2001) (Published by The Ecstatic Exchange, 2007)
Where Death Goes (9/20/2001 – 5/1/2002)
The Flame of Transformation Turns to Light (99 Ghazals Written in English) (5/14
    – 8/21/2002) (Published by The Ecstatic Exchange, 2007)
Through Rose-Colored Glasses (7/22/2002 – 1/15/2003) (Published by The Ecstatic
    Exchange, 2008)
Psalms for the Broken-Hearted (1/22 – 5/25/2003) (Published by The Ecstatic
    Exchange, 2006)
Hoopoe's Argument (5/27 – 9/18/03)
Love is a Letter Burning in a High Wind (9/21 – 11/6/2003) (Published by The
    Ecstatic Exchange, 2006)
Laughing Buddha/Weeping Sufi(11/7/2003 – 1/10/2004) (Published
    by The Ecstatic Exchange, 2005)
Mars and Beyond (1/20 – 3/29/2004) (Published by The Ecstatic Exchange, 2005)
Underwater Galaxies (4/5 – 7/21/2004) (Published by The Ecstatic Exchange, 2007)
Cooked Oranges (7/23/2004 – 1/24/2005 (Published by The Ecstatic Exchange,
    2007)
Holiday from the Perfect Crime (1/25 – 6/11/2005)
Stories Too Fiery to Sing Too Watery to Whisper (6/13 – 10/24/2005)
Coattails of the Saint (10/26/2005 – 5/10/2006) (Published by The Ecstatic
    Exchange, 2006)
In the Realm of Neither (5/14/2006 – 11/12/06)
Invention of the Wheel (11/13/06 – 6/10/07)
The Sound of Geese Over the House (6/15 – 11/4/07)
The Fire Eater's Lunchbreak / Tall Tales in Short Takes (11/10/07 –)

www.ingramcontent.com/pod-product-compliance
Lightning Source LLC
Chambersburg PA
CBHW031846090426
42741CB00005B/375